Written and Illustrated by

Kanban Studio

Kanban's Sexy Fighters - Full Color! © 2020 Kanban Studio

All Artwork © 2010 -2020 Kanban Studio

All characters tm and © 2010-2020 of their respective holders

Any ommission or incorrect information should be transmitted to the author or the publisher so it can be rectified in future edition of this book.

No part of this book may be used or reproduced in any manner whatsoever without written permission except in the case of brief quotations embodied in critical articles and reviews.

Kanban's Sexy Fighters

Full Color!

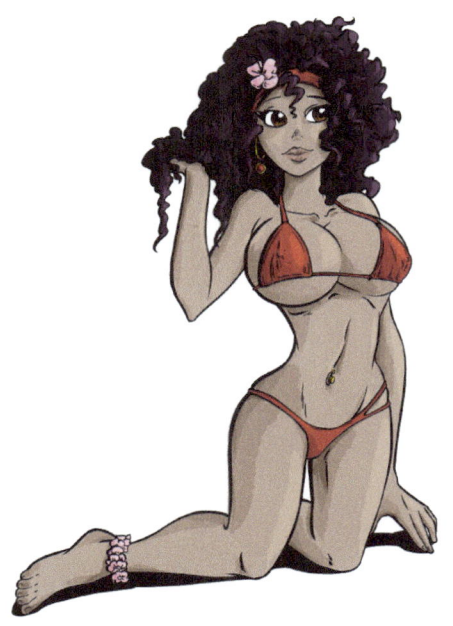

by Kanban Studio

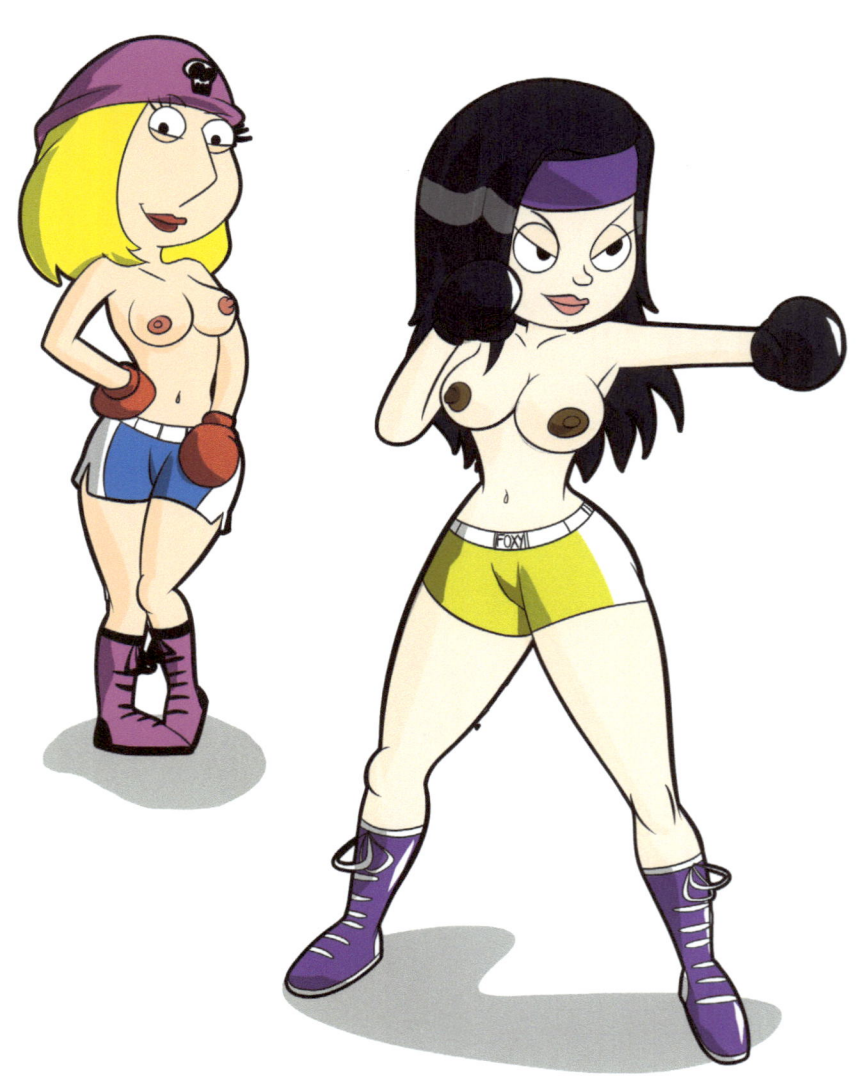

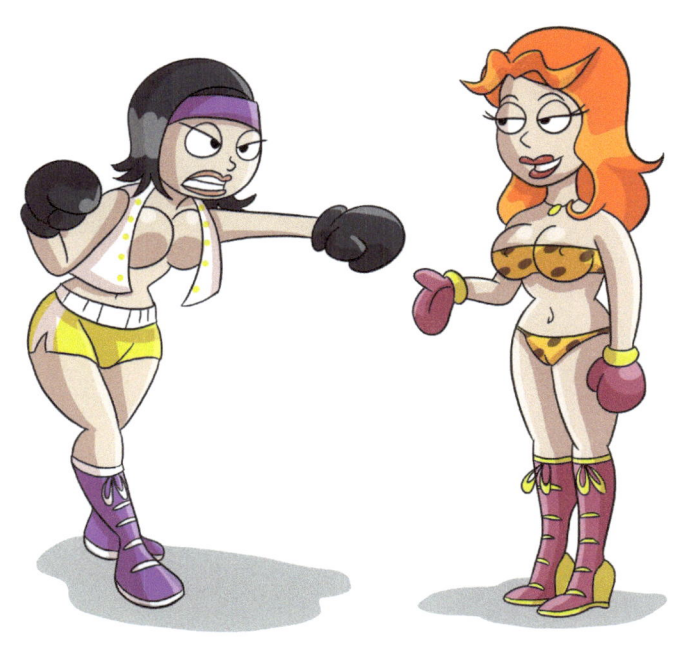
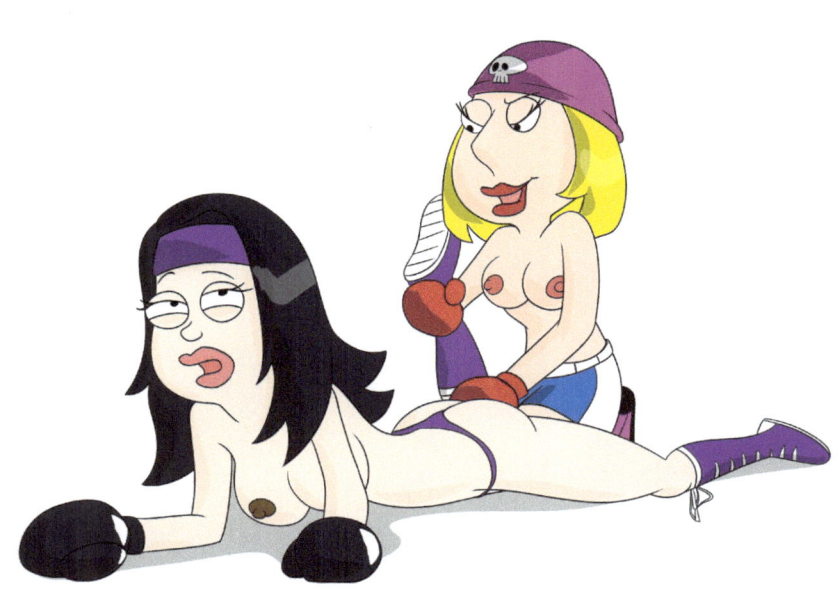

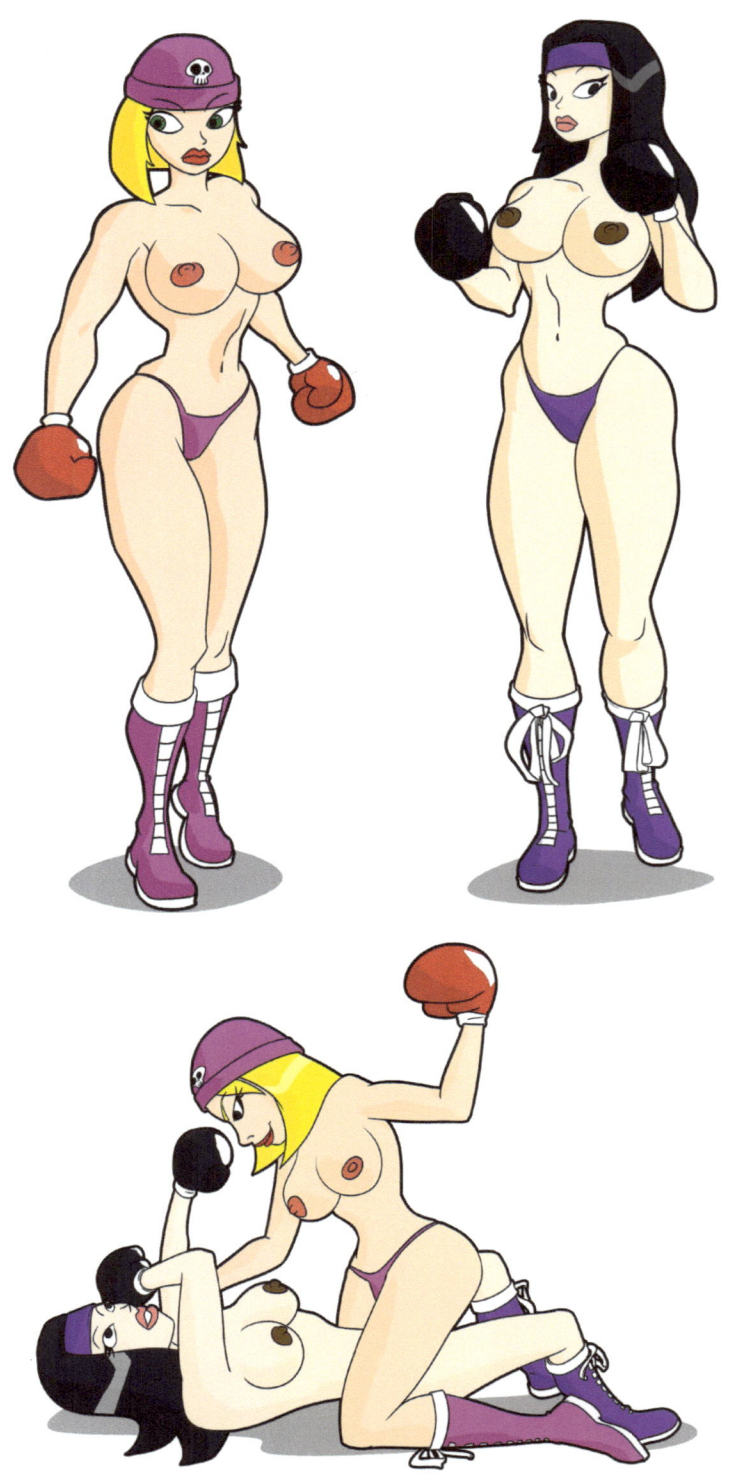

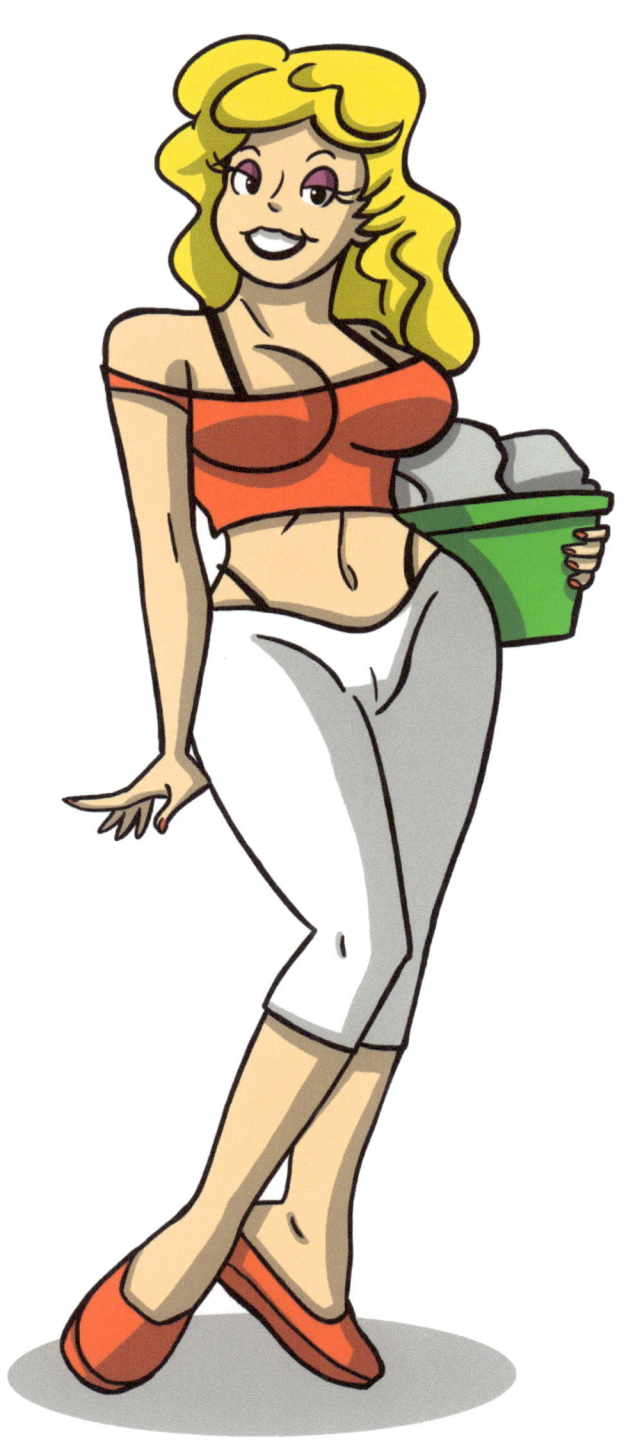

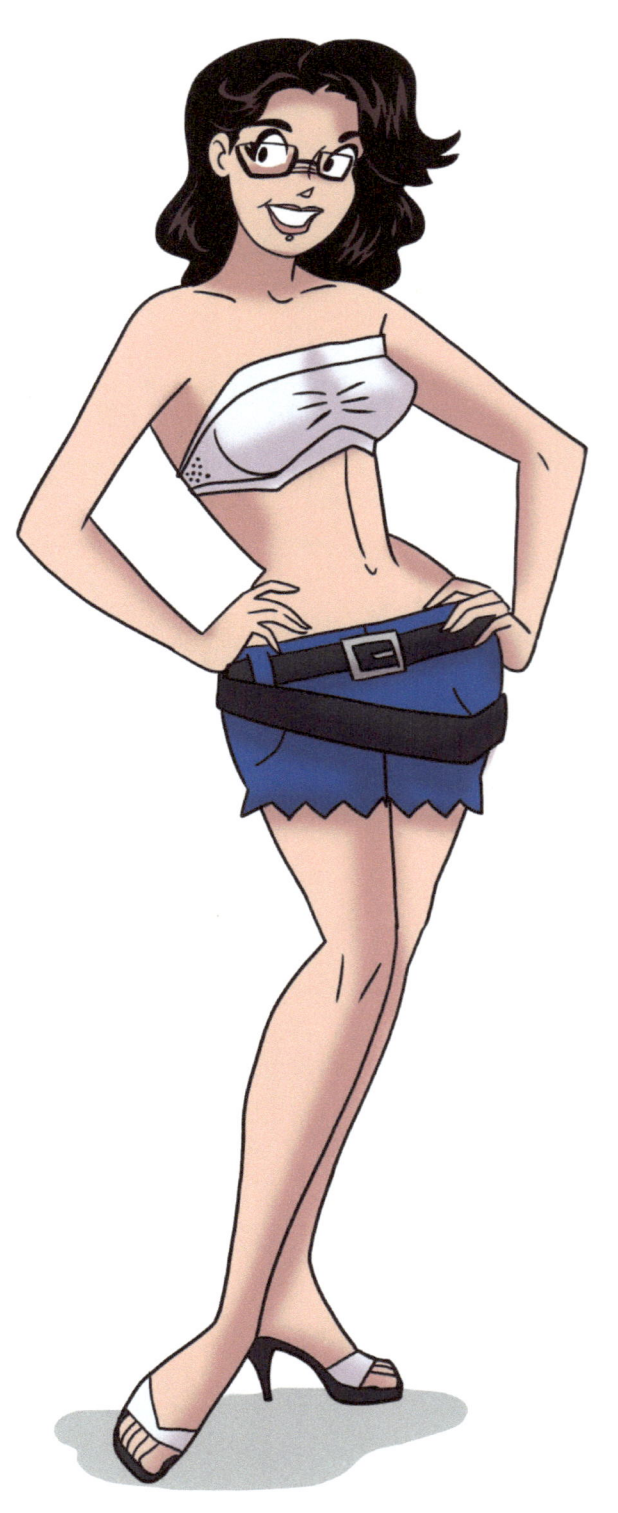

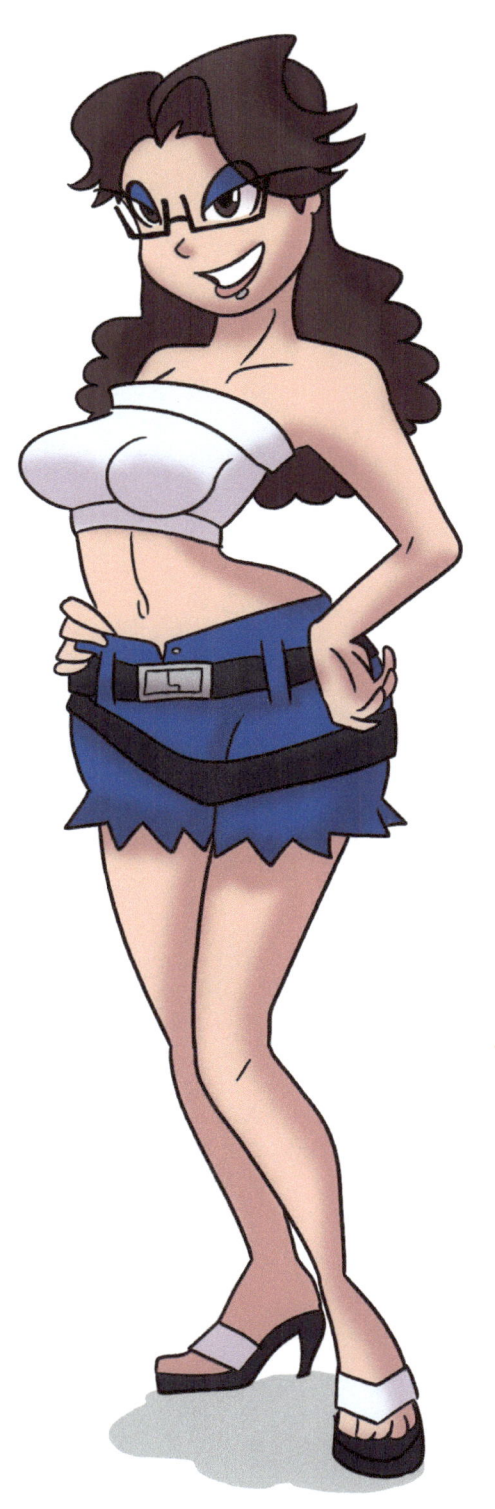

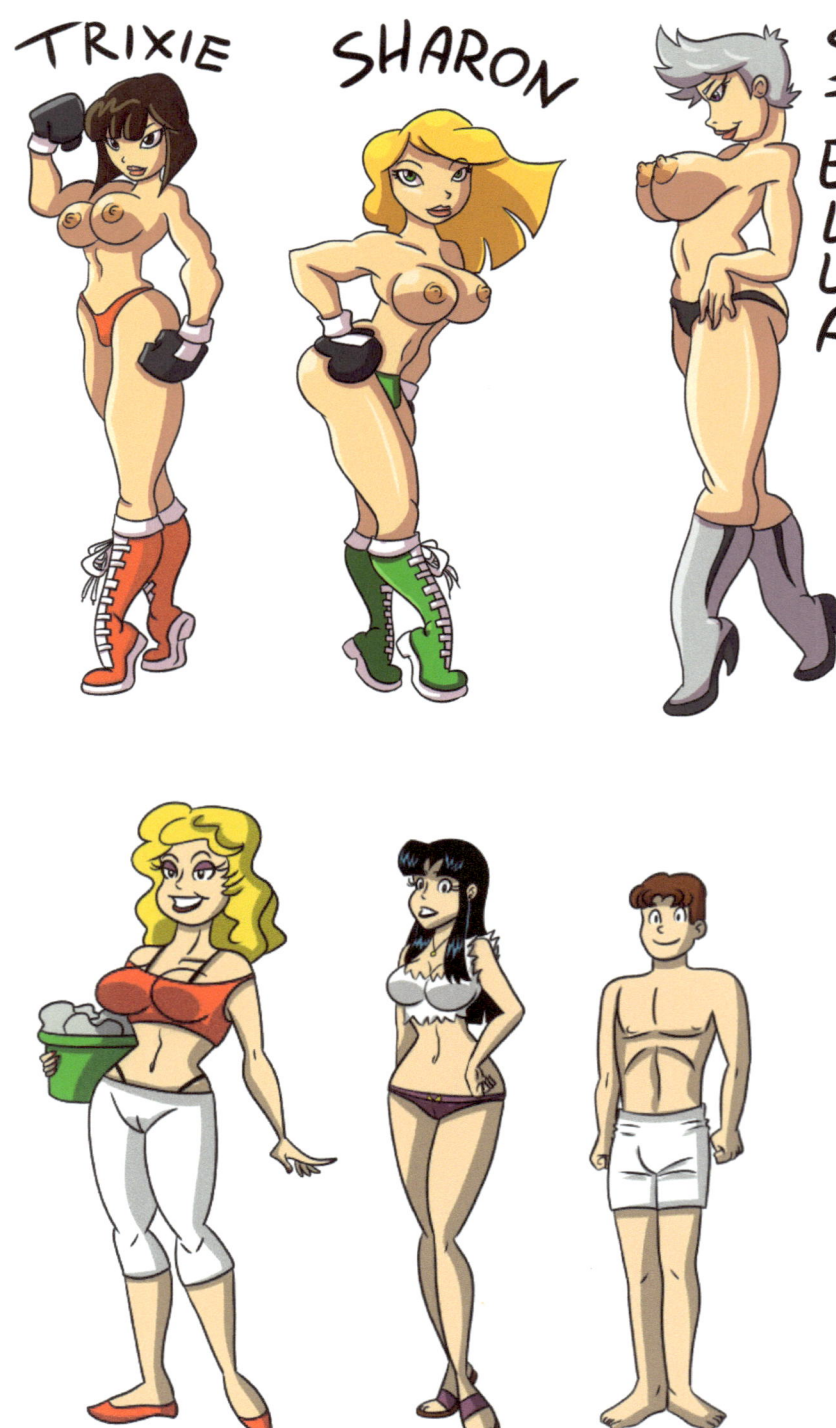

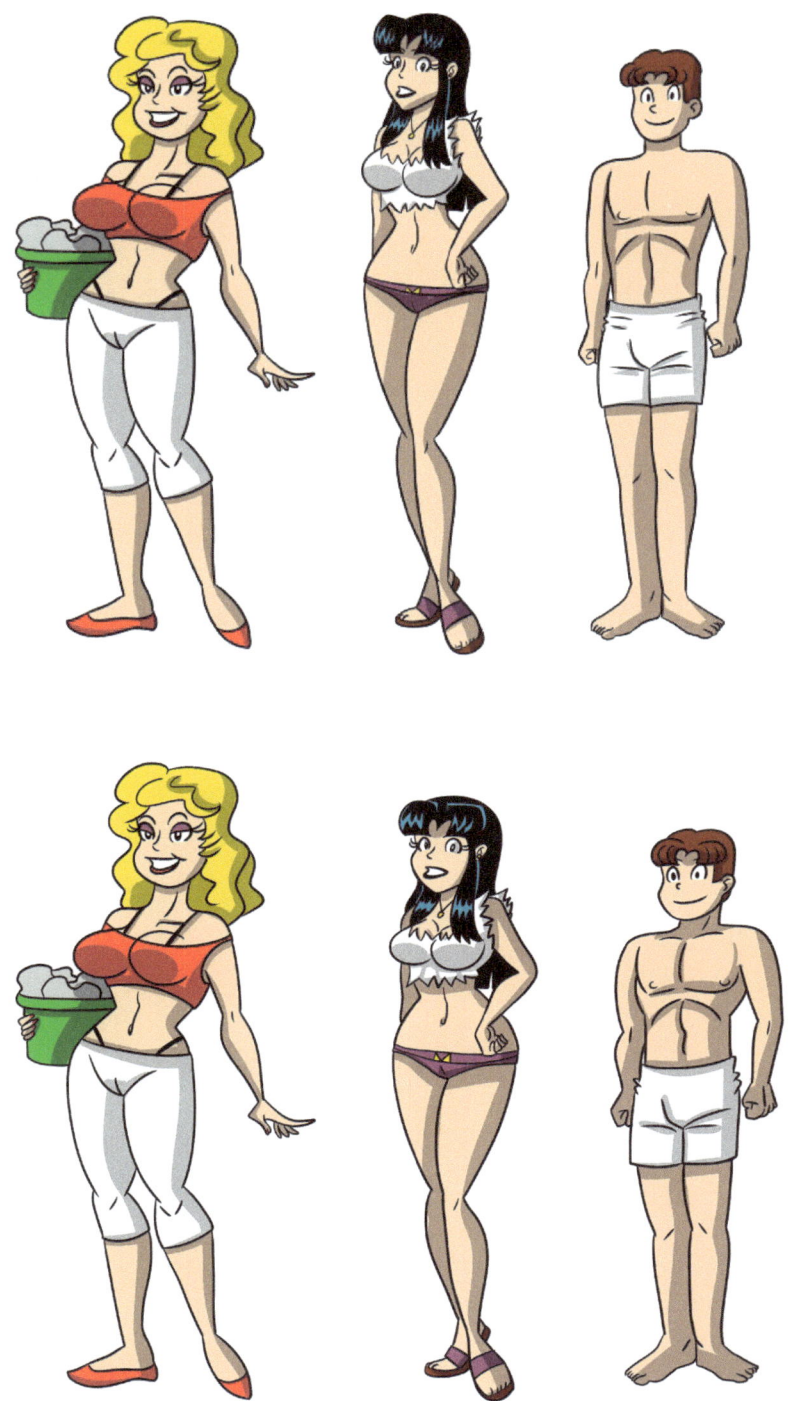

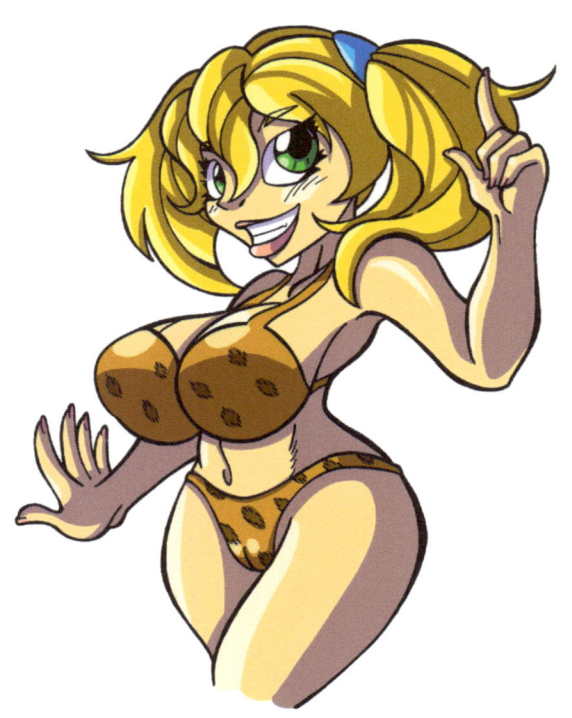

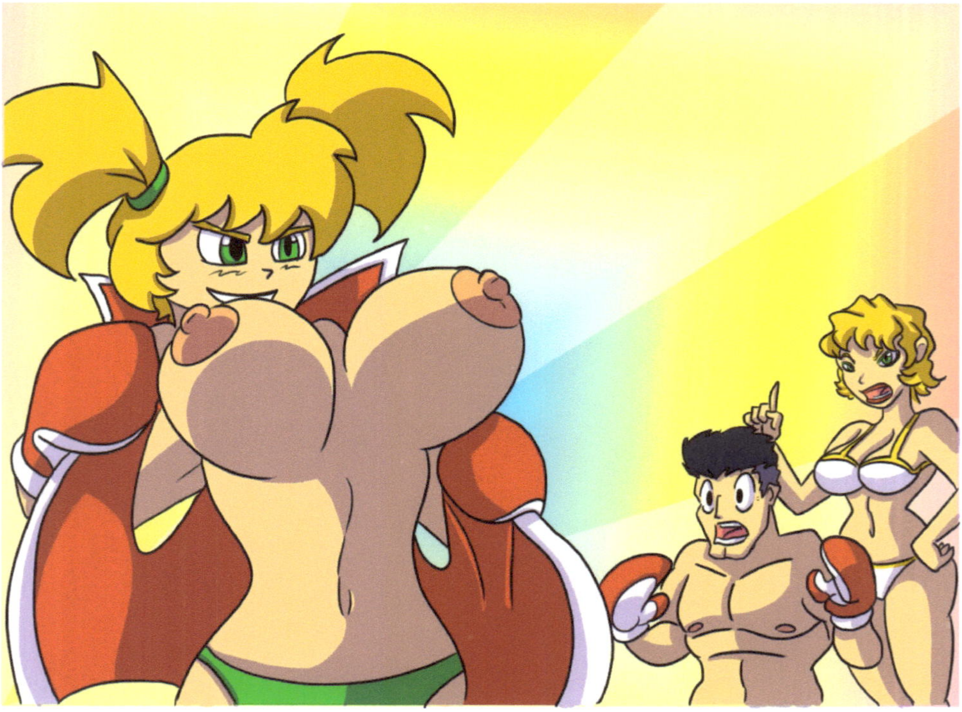

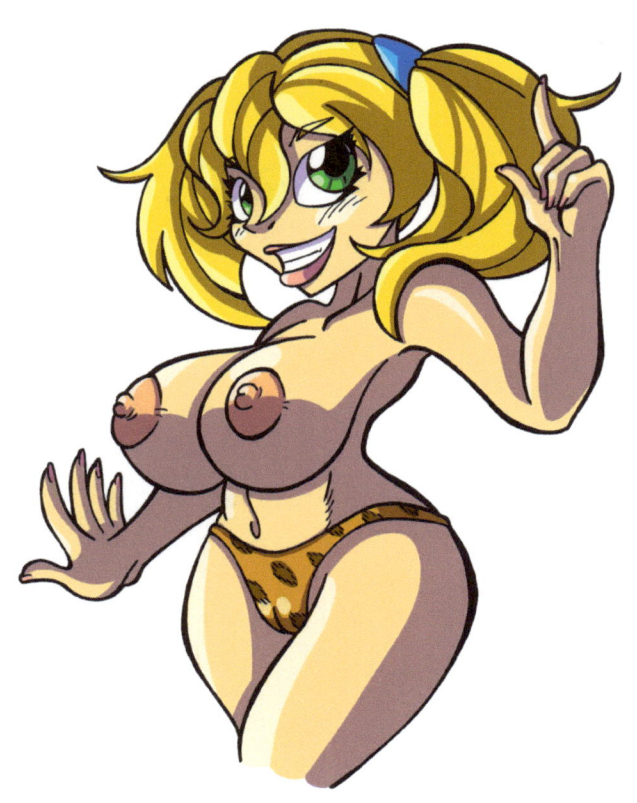
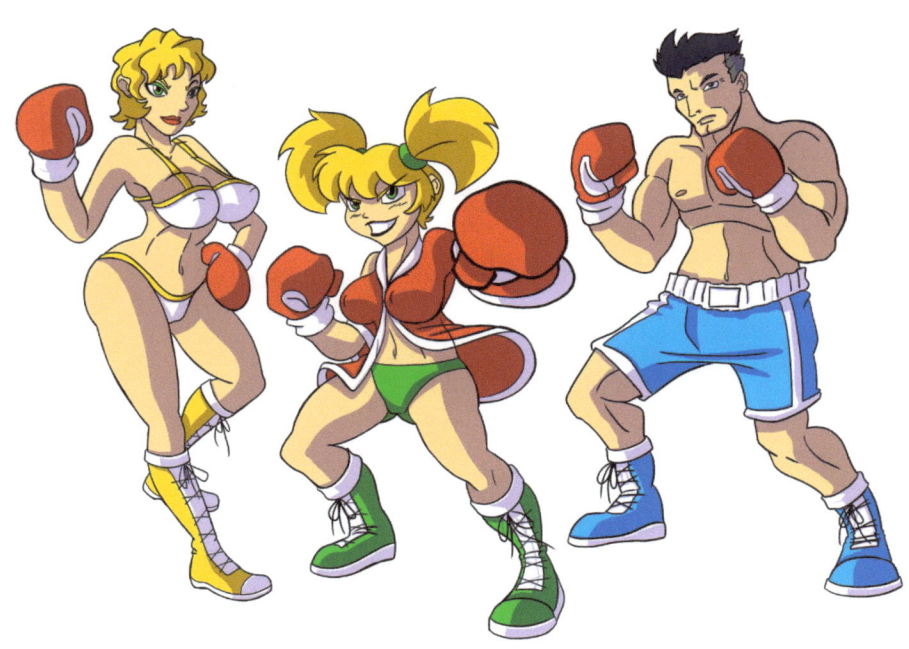

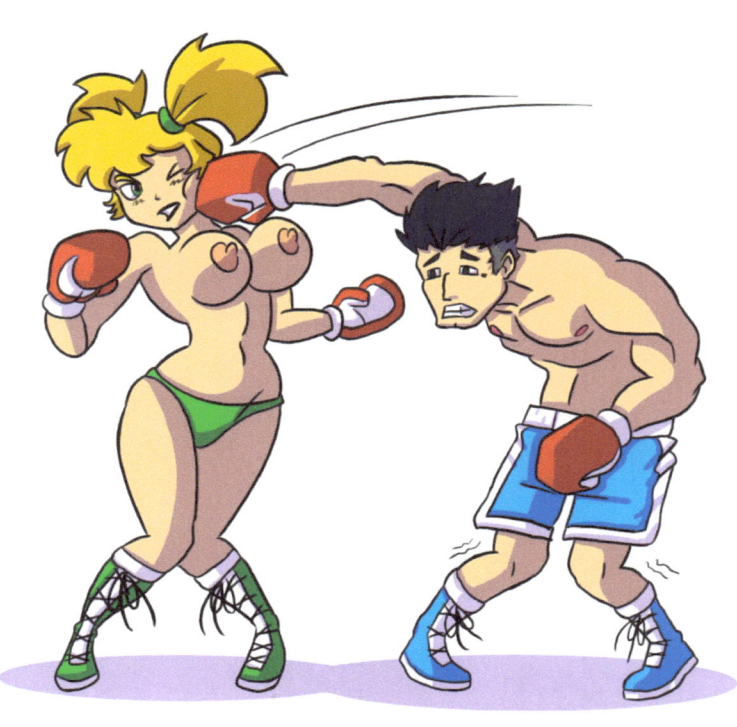

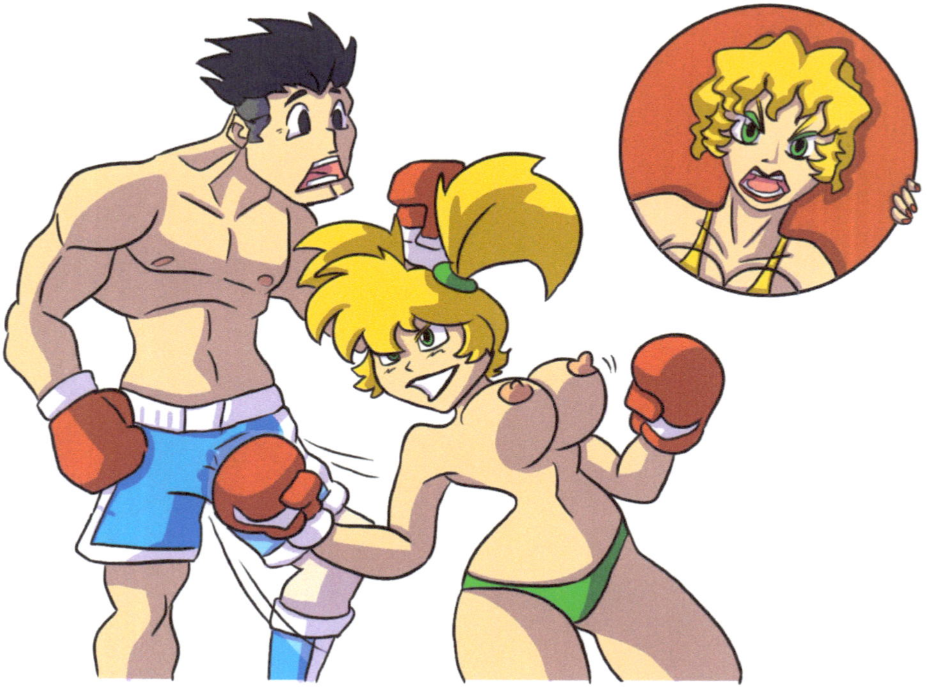

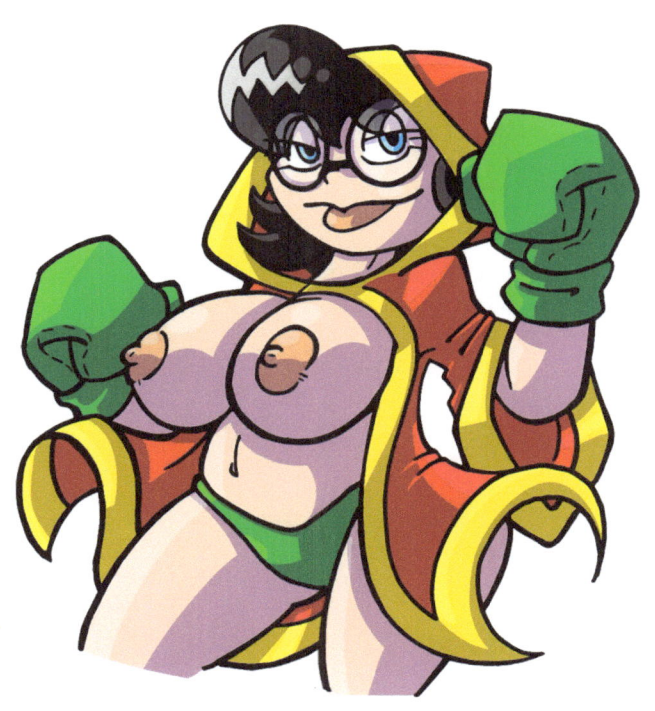
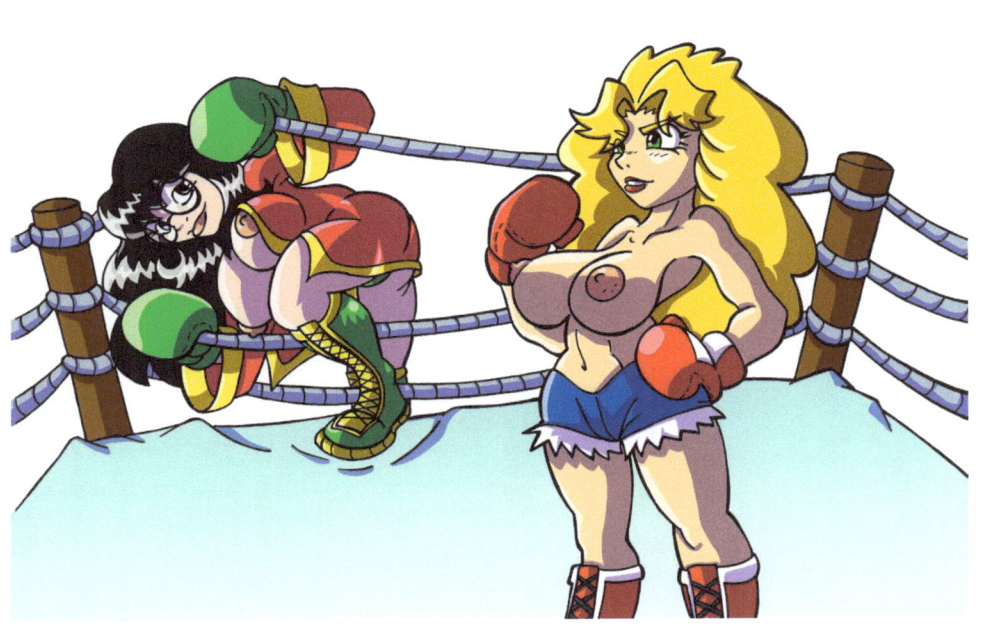

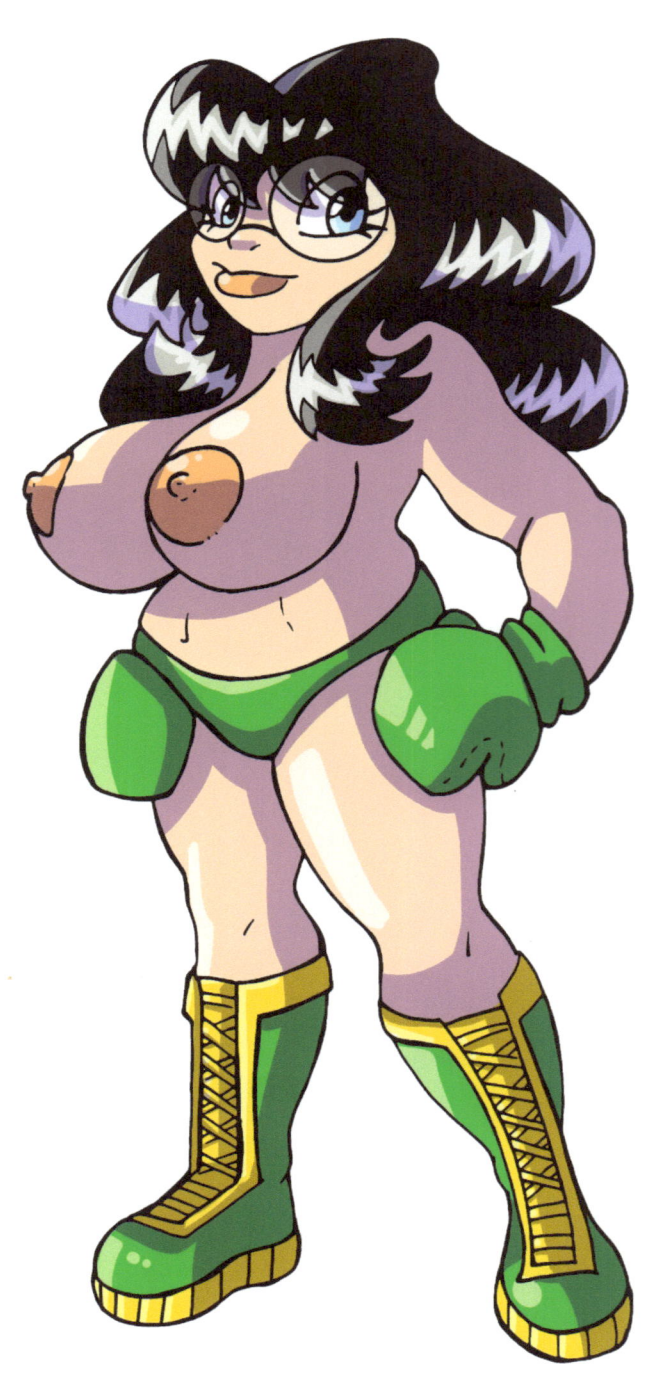

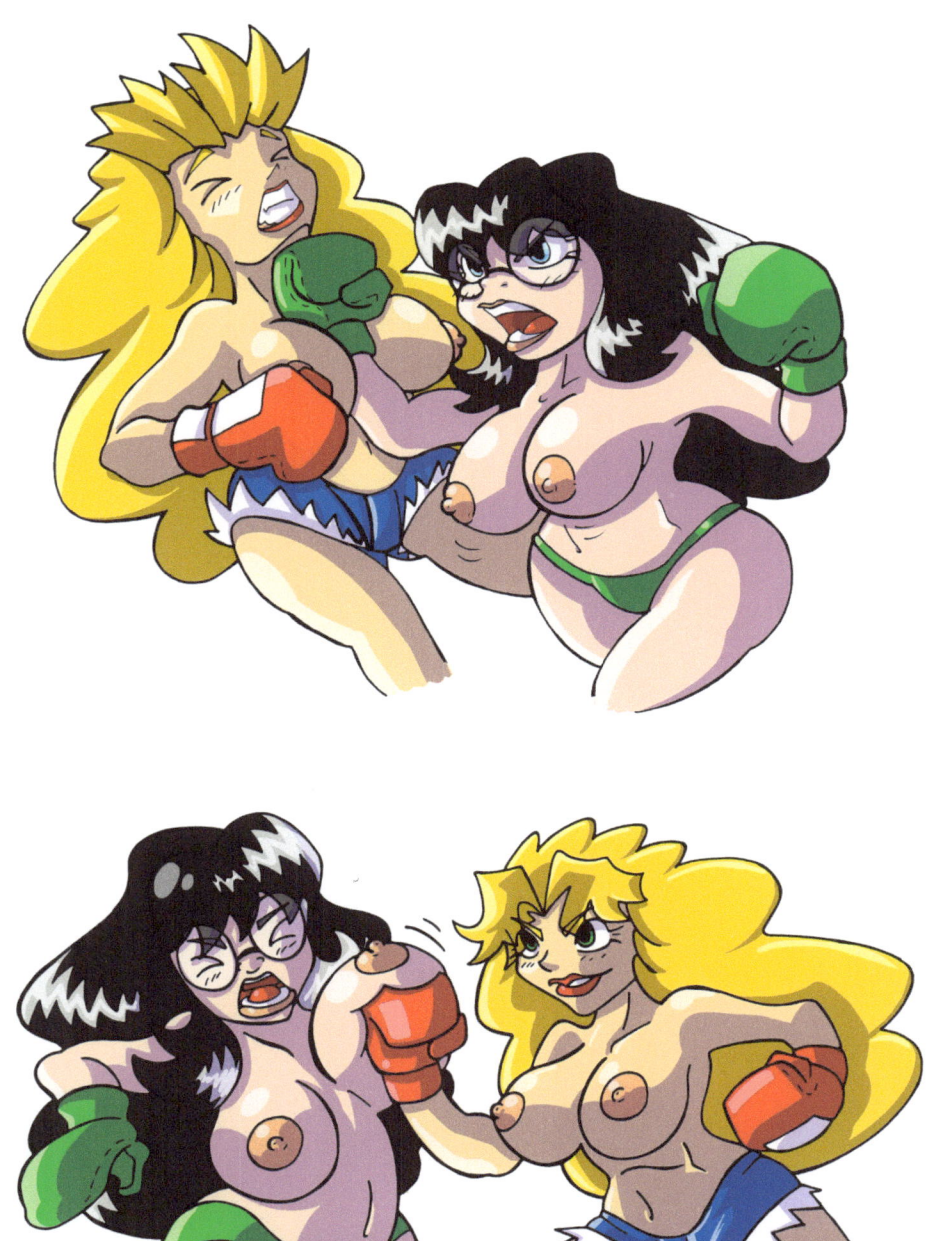

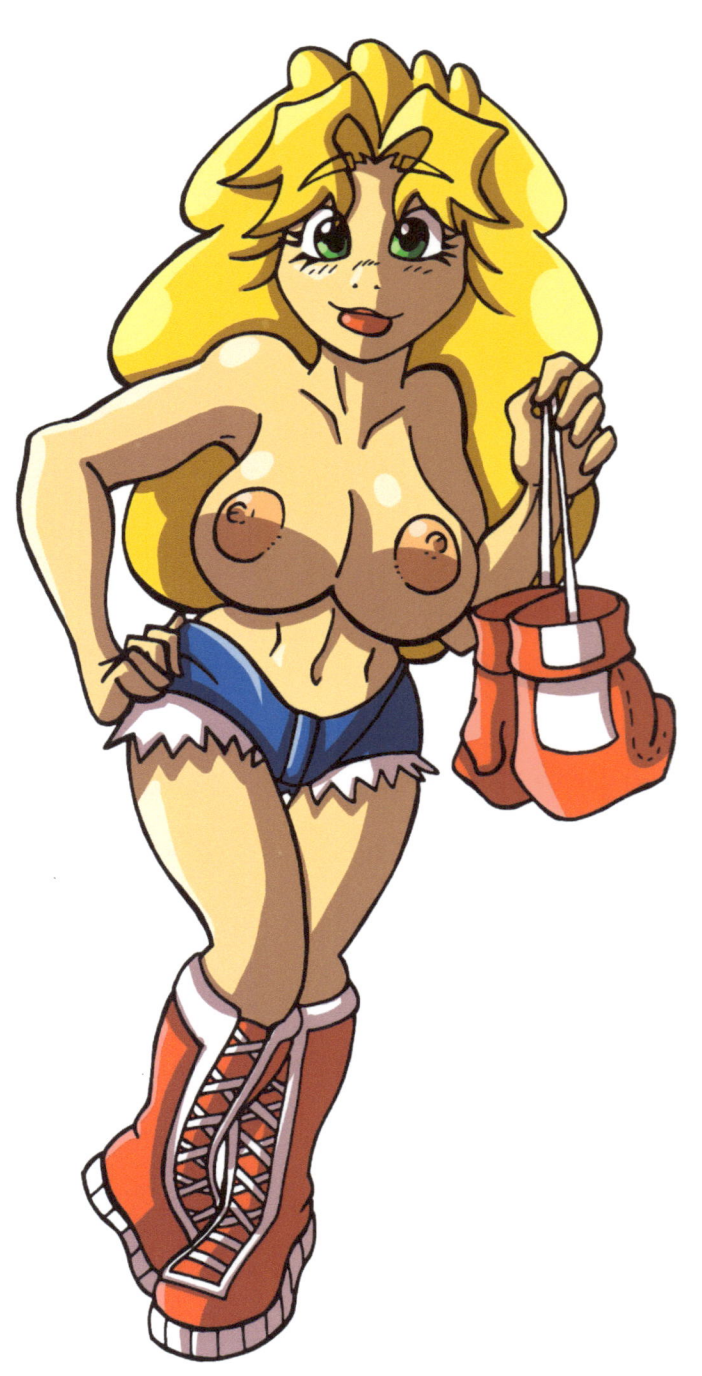

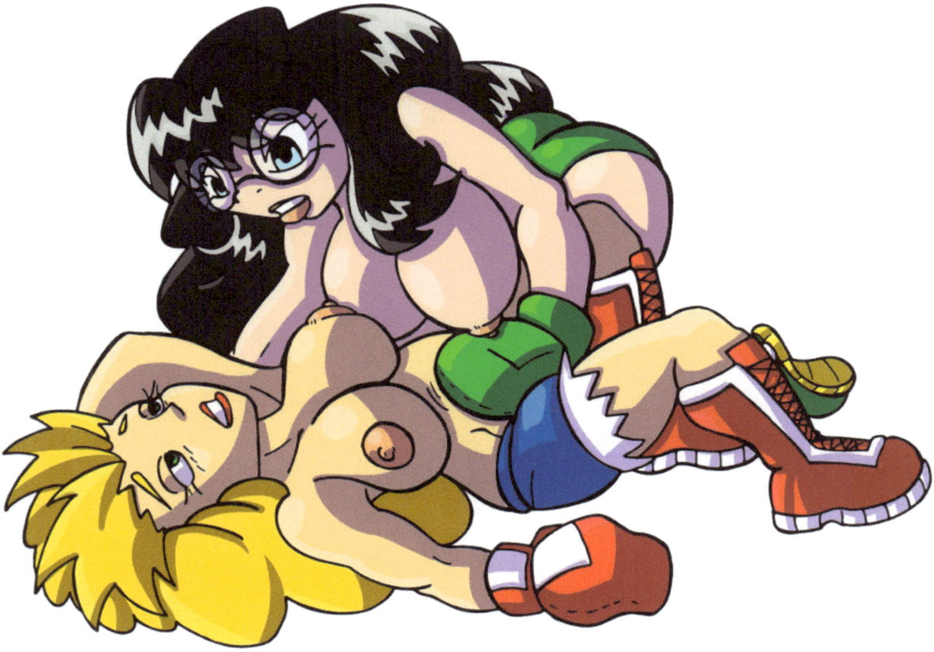

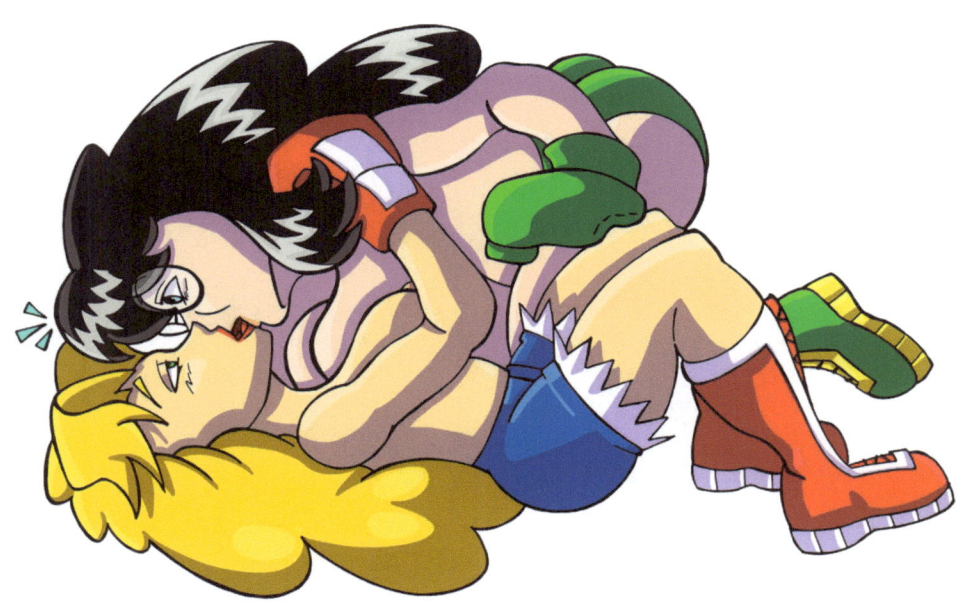

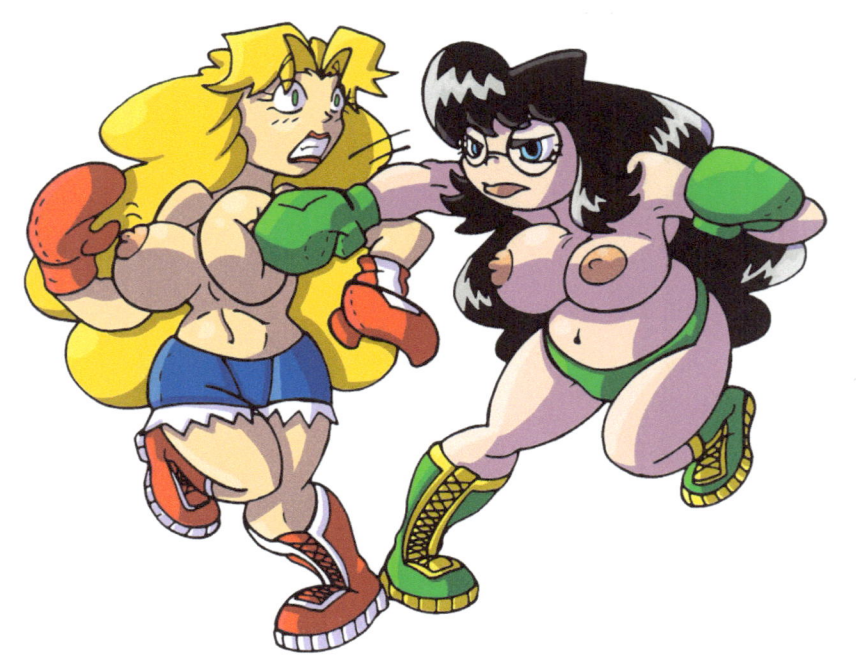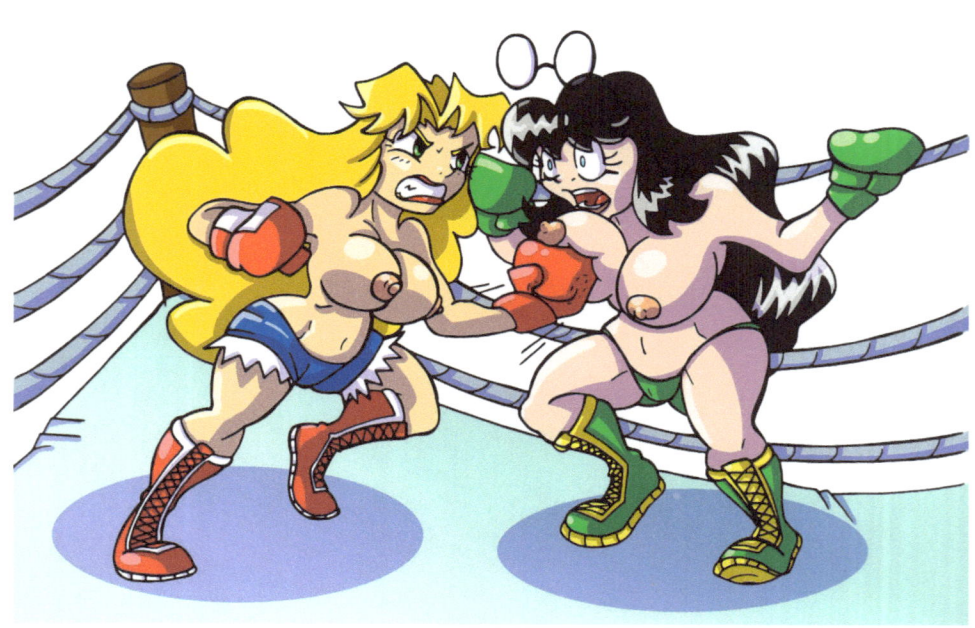

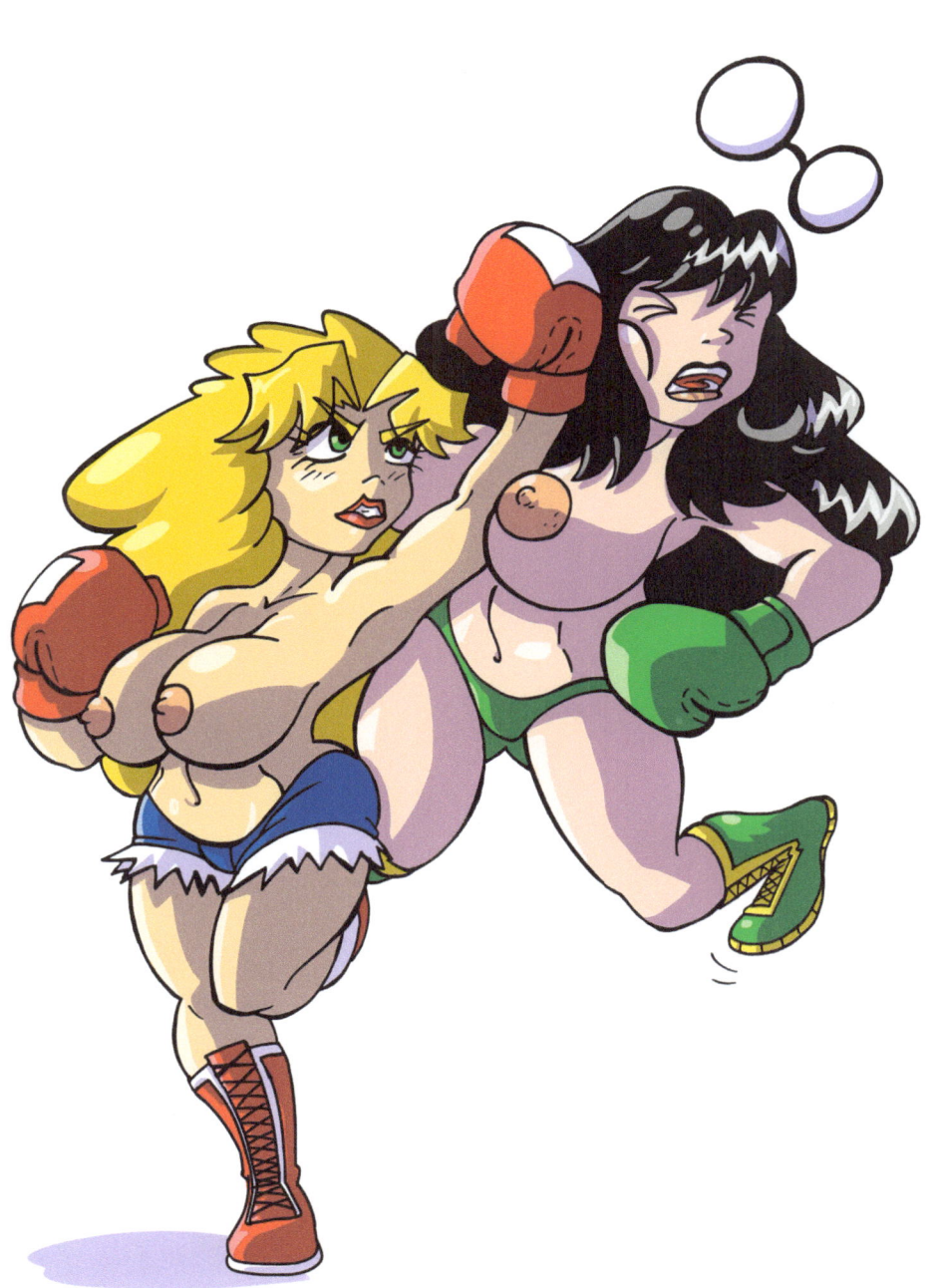

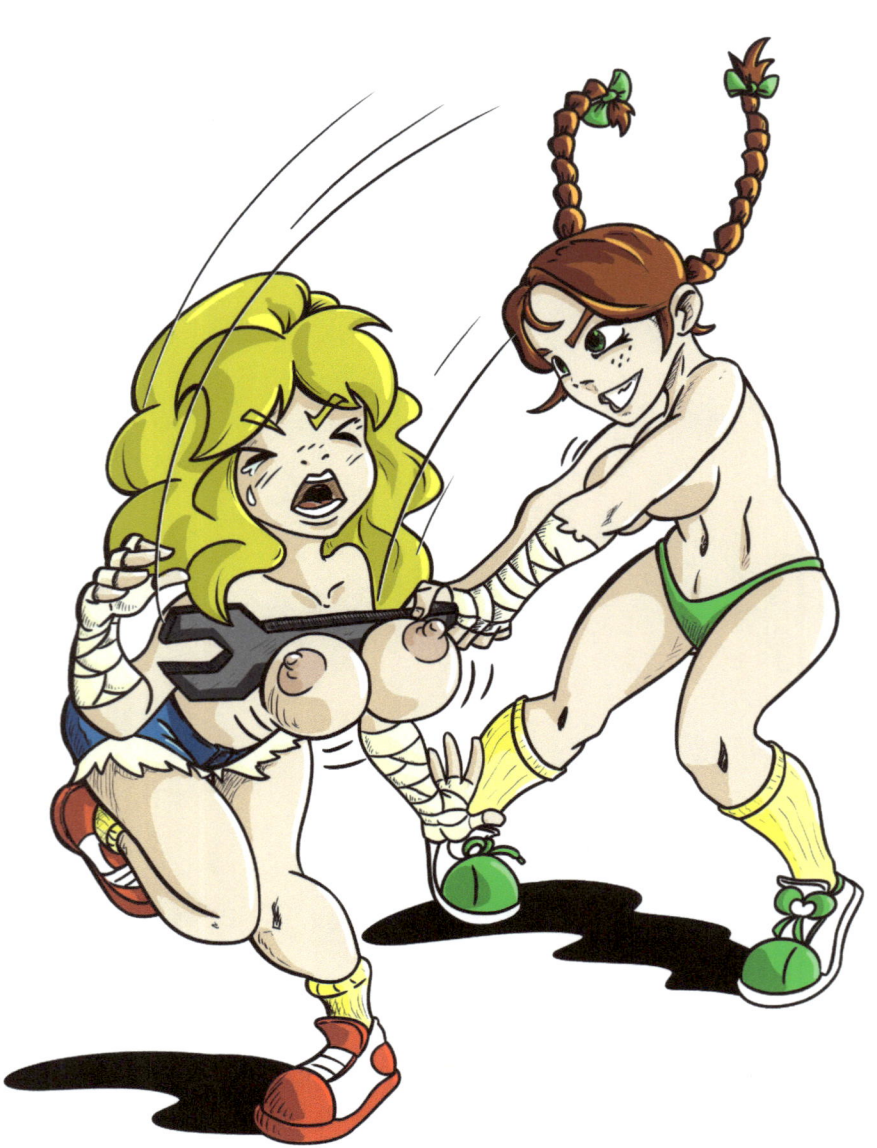

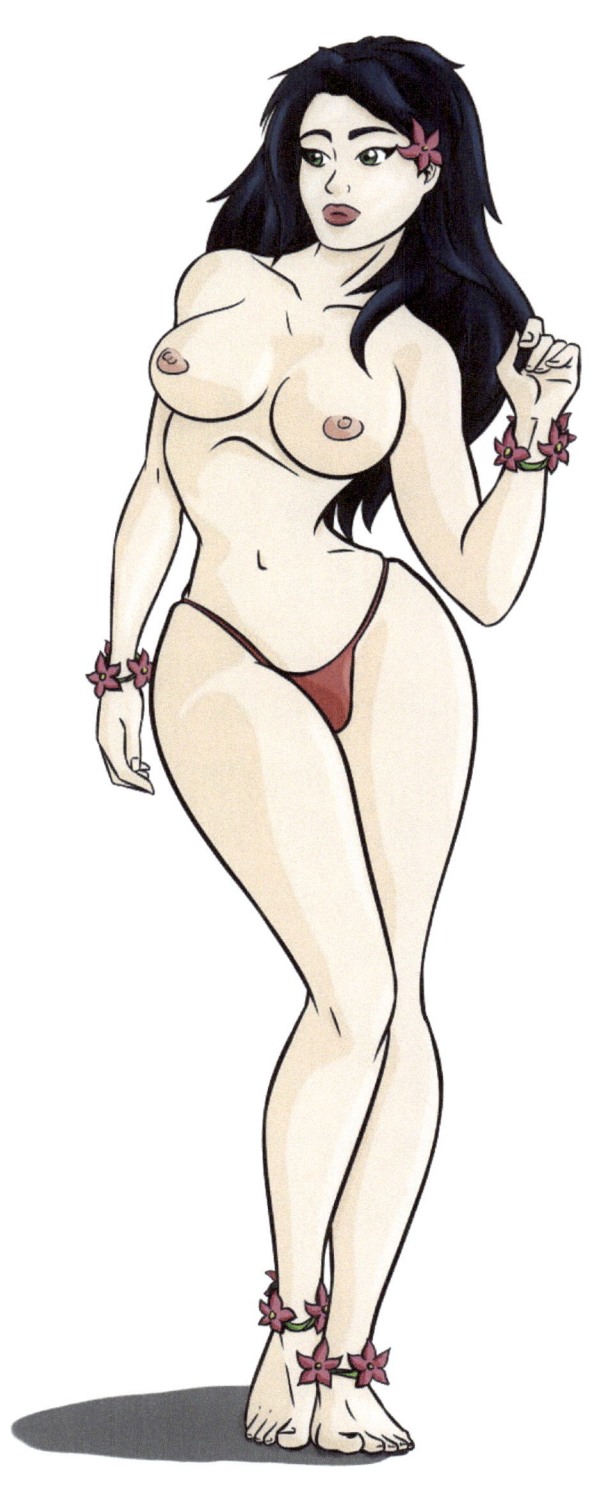

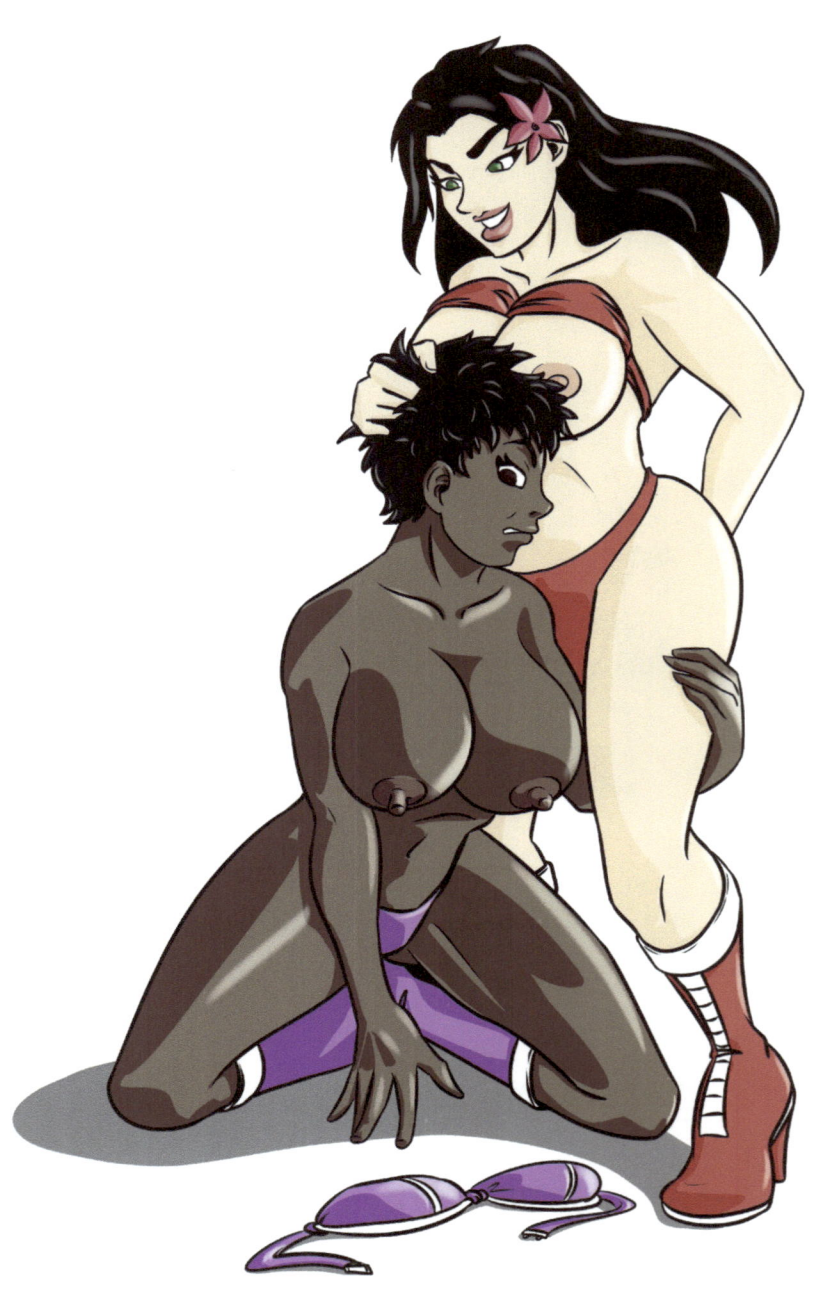

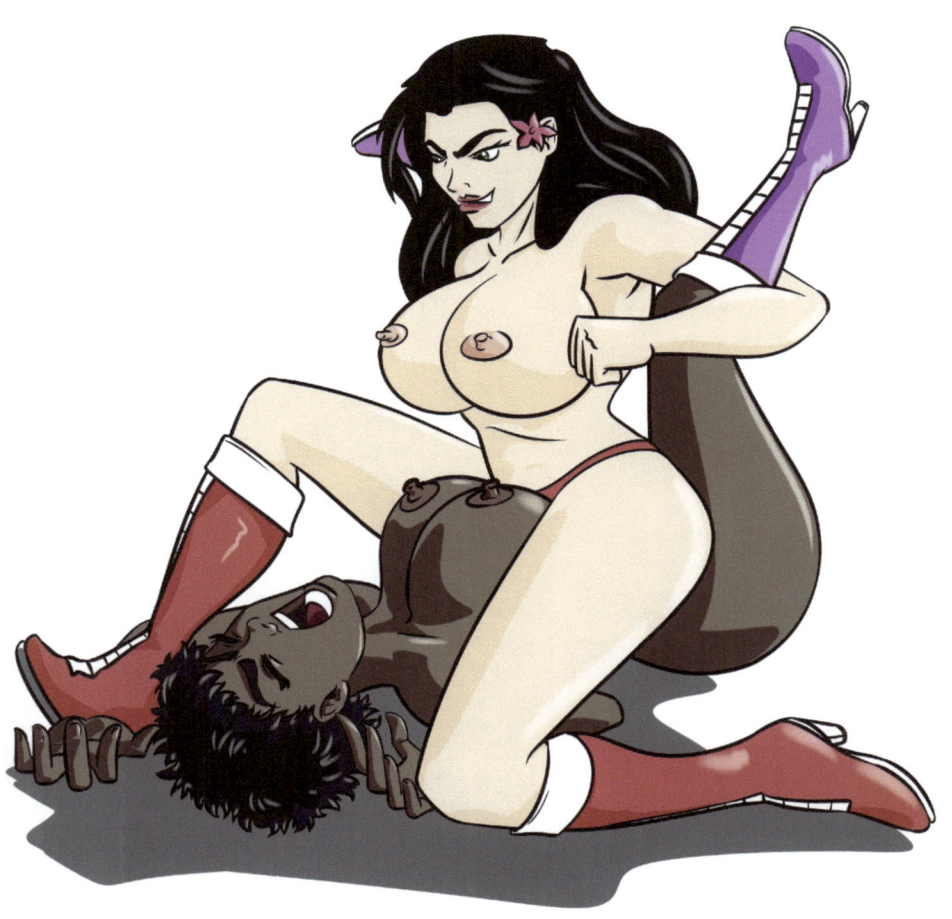

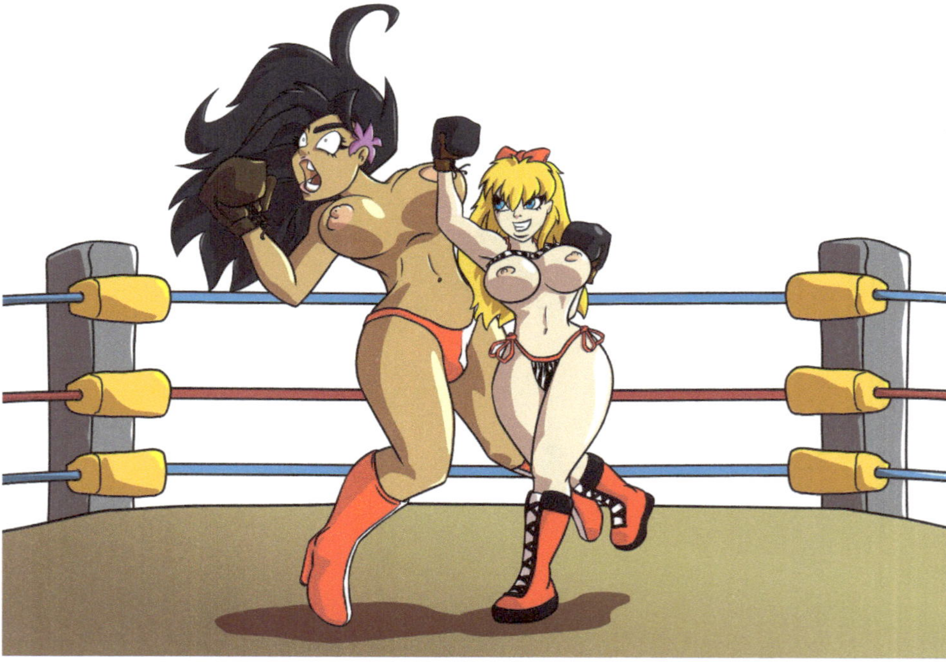

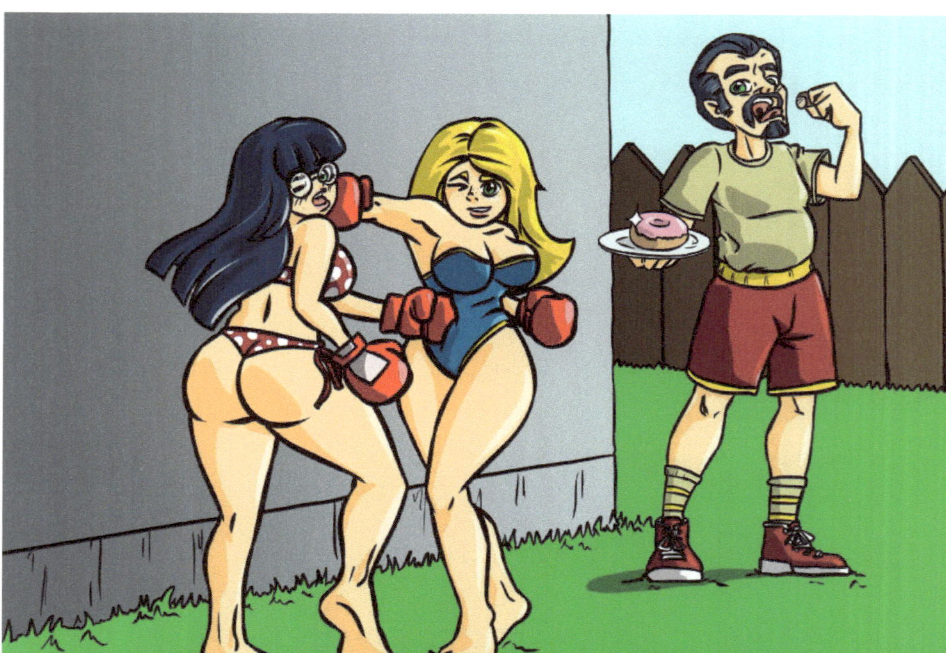

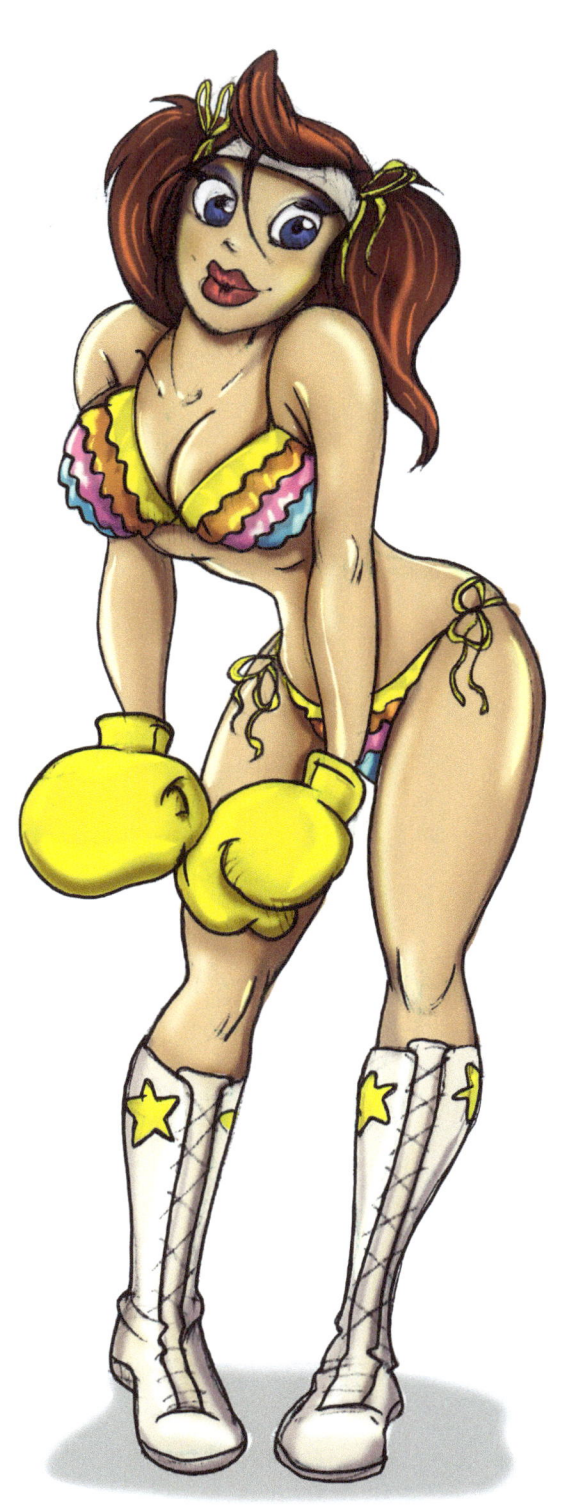

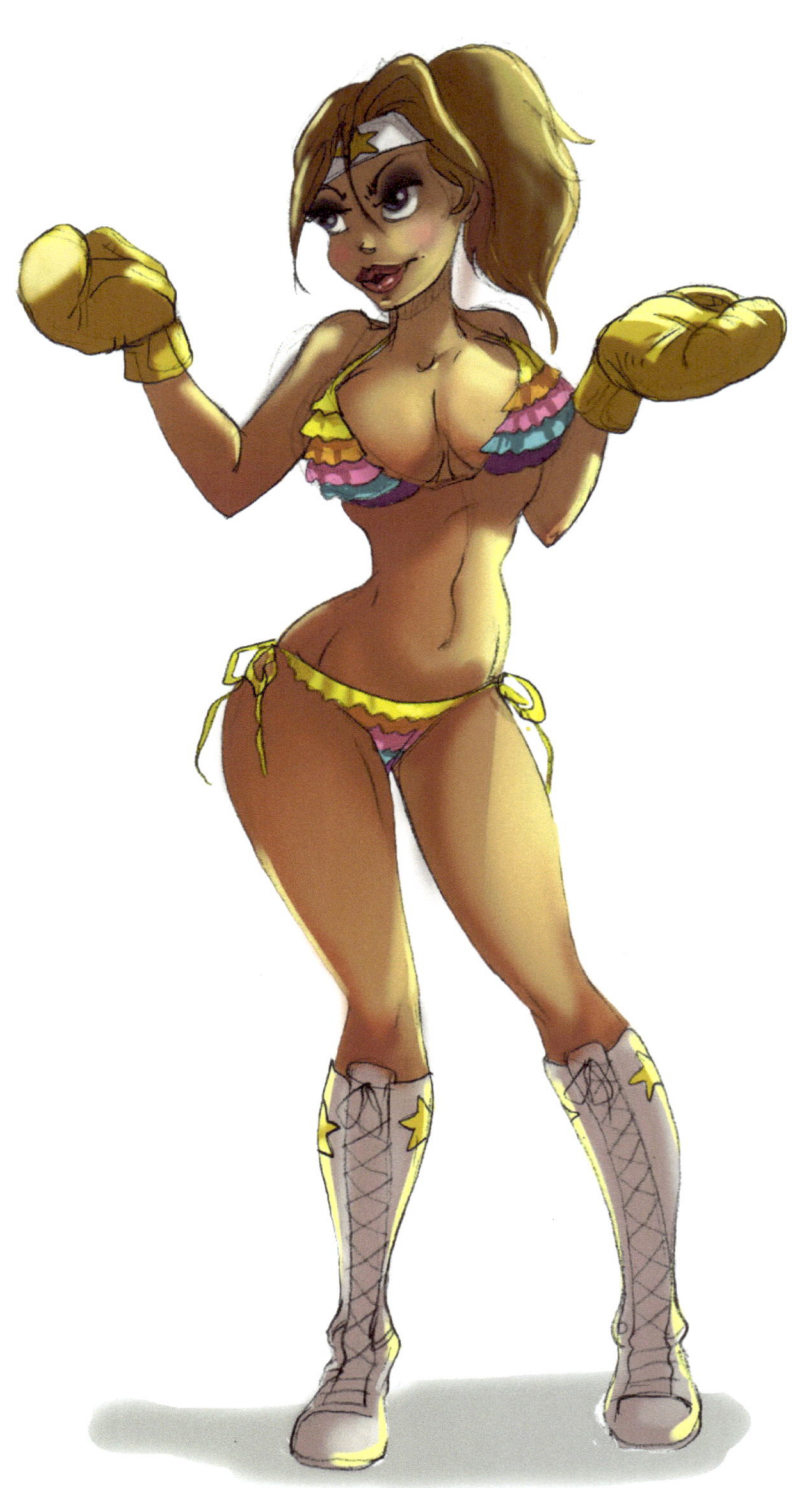

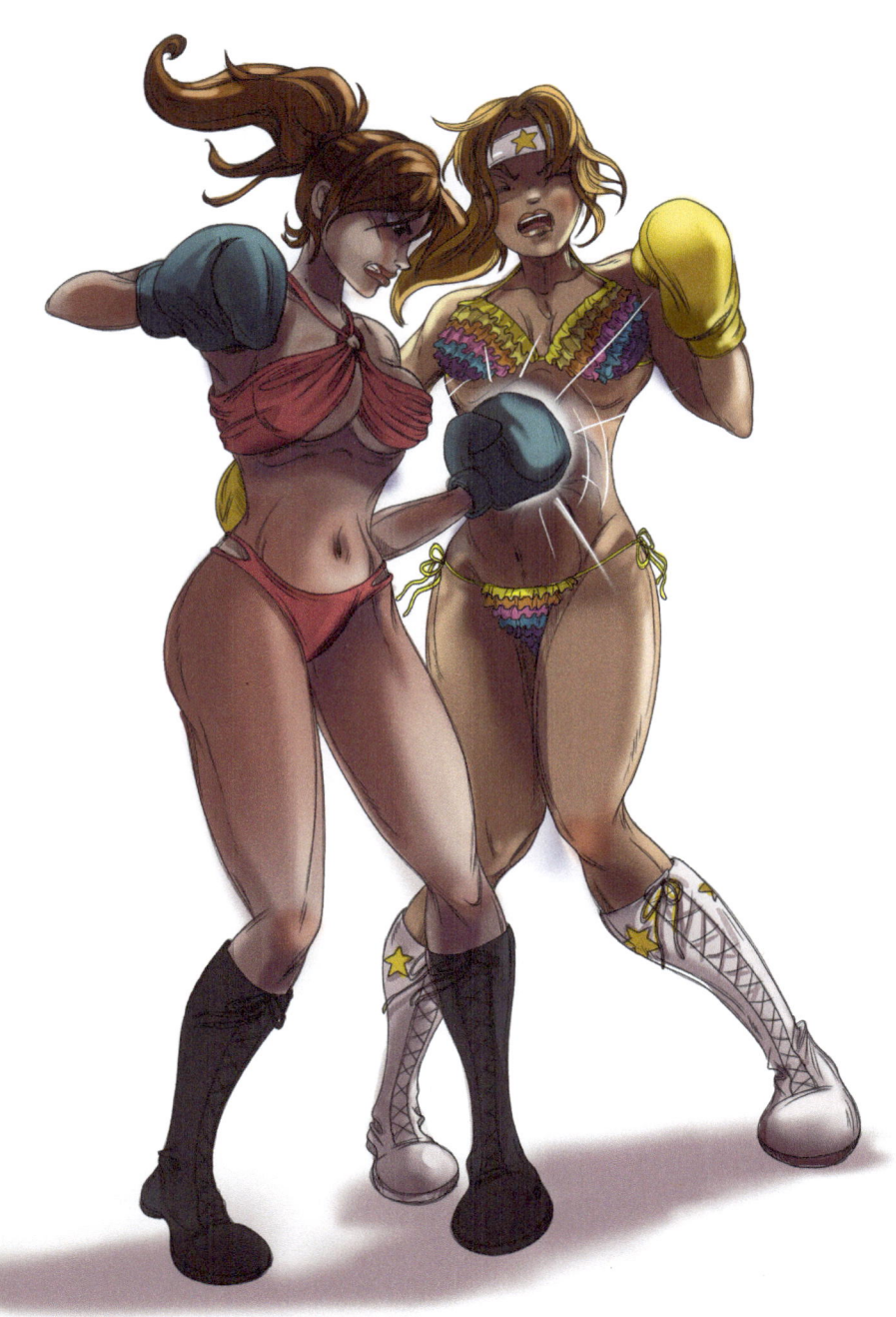

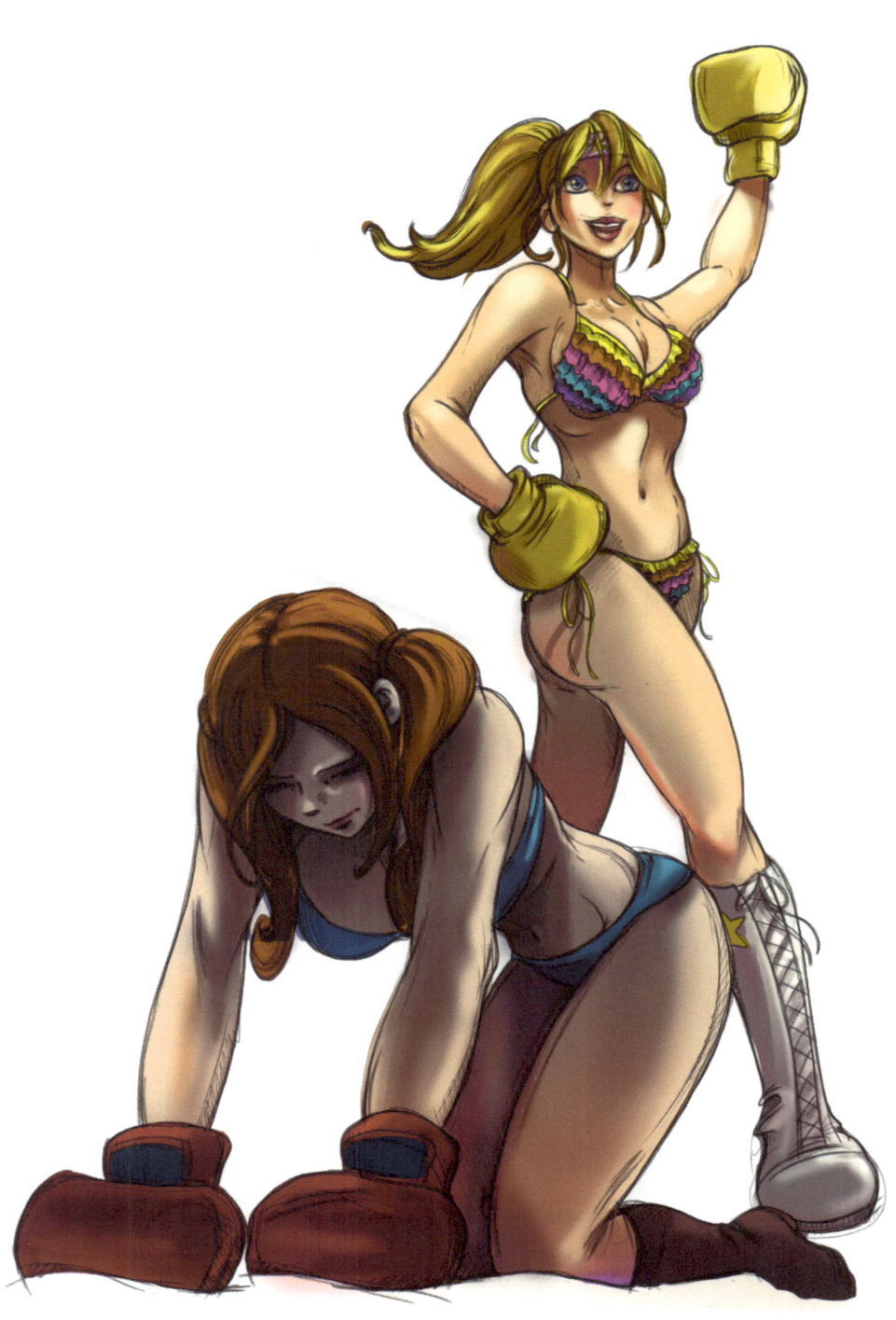

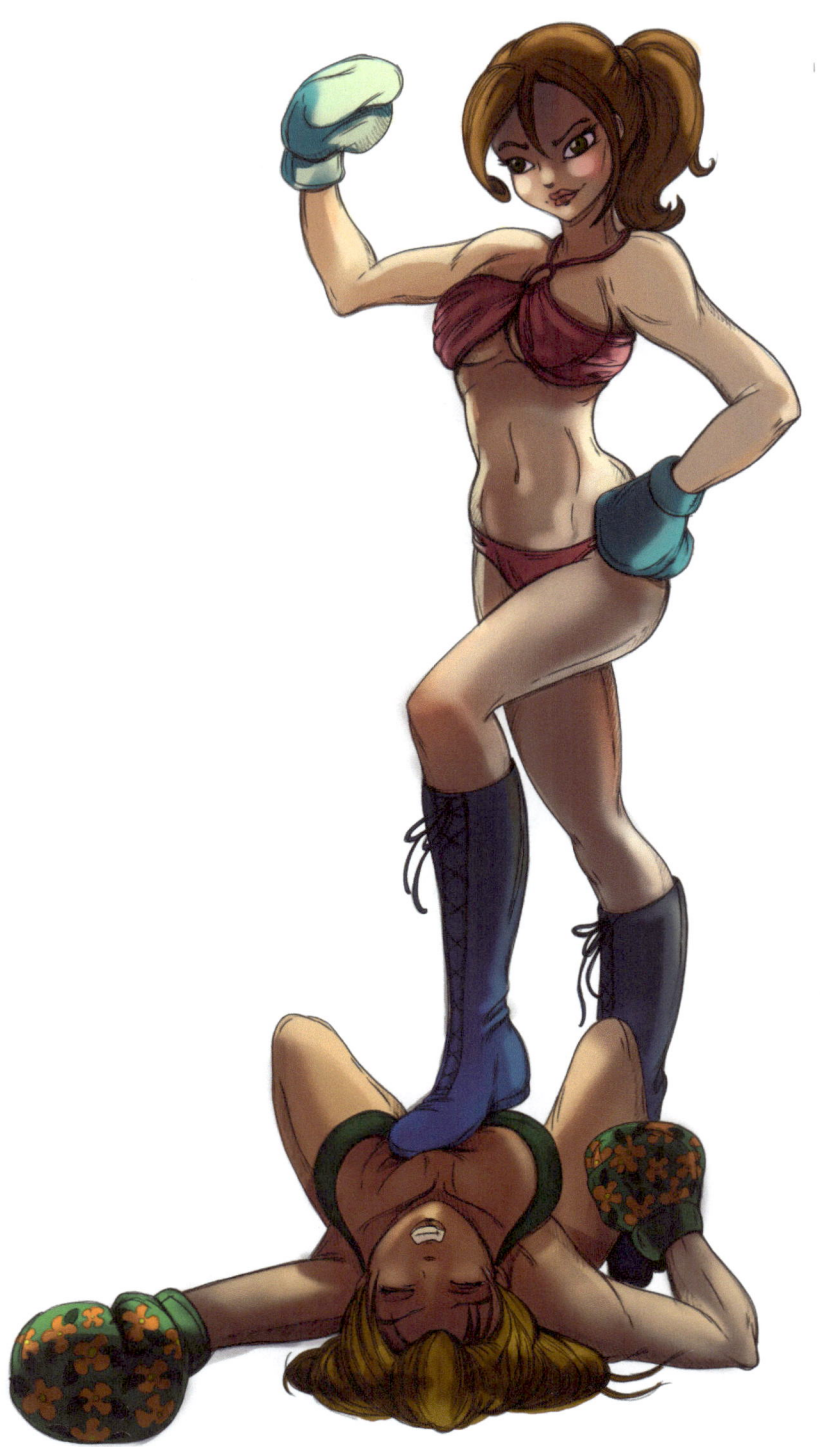

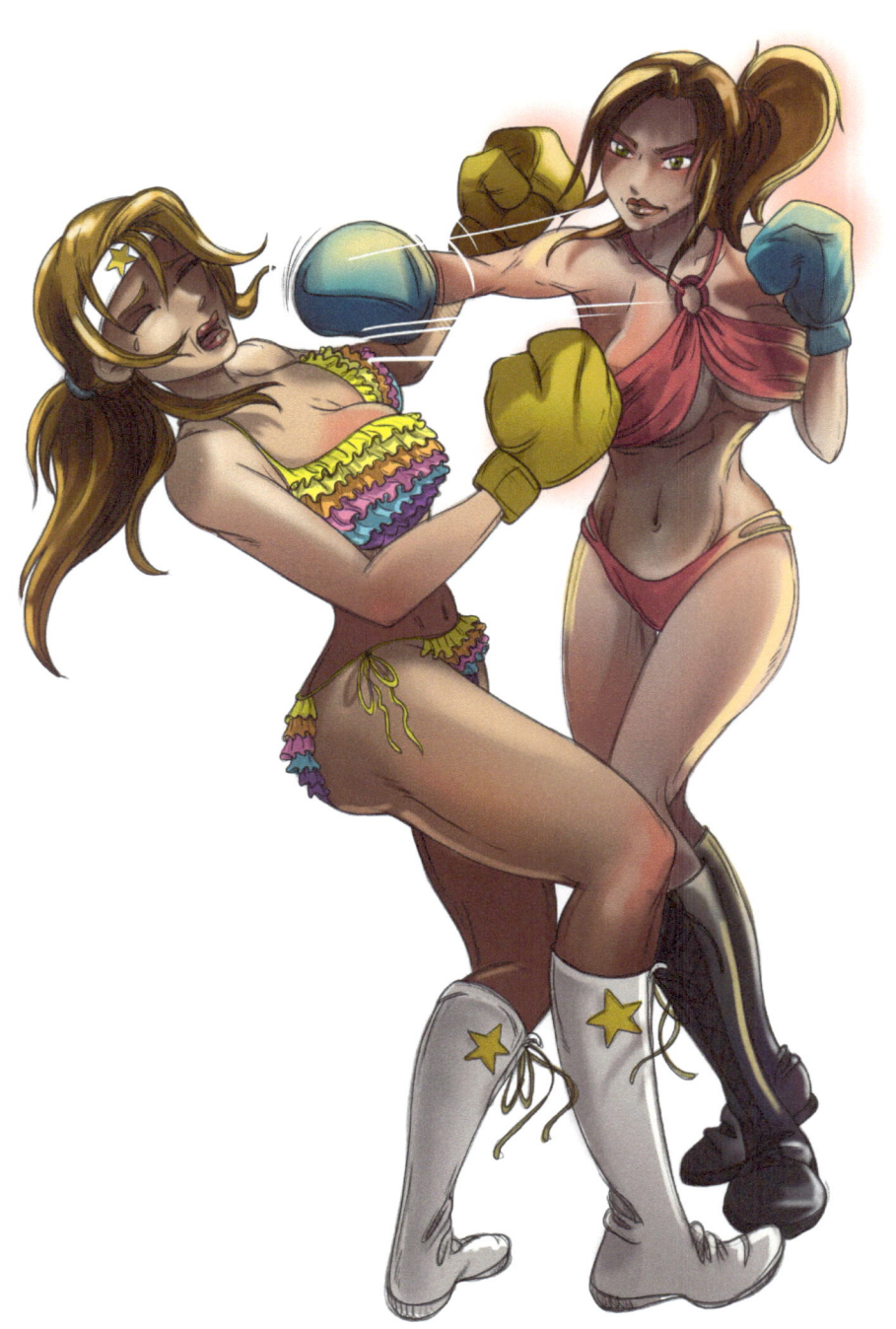

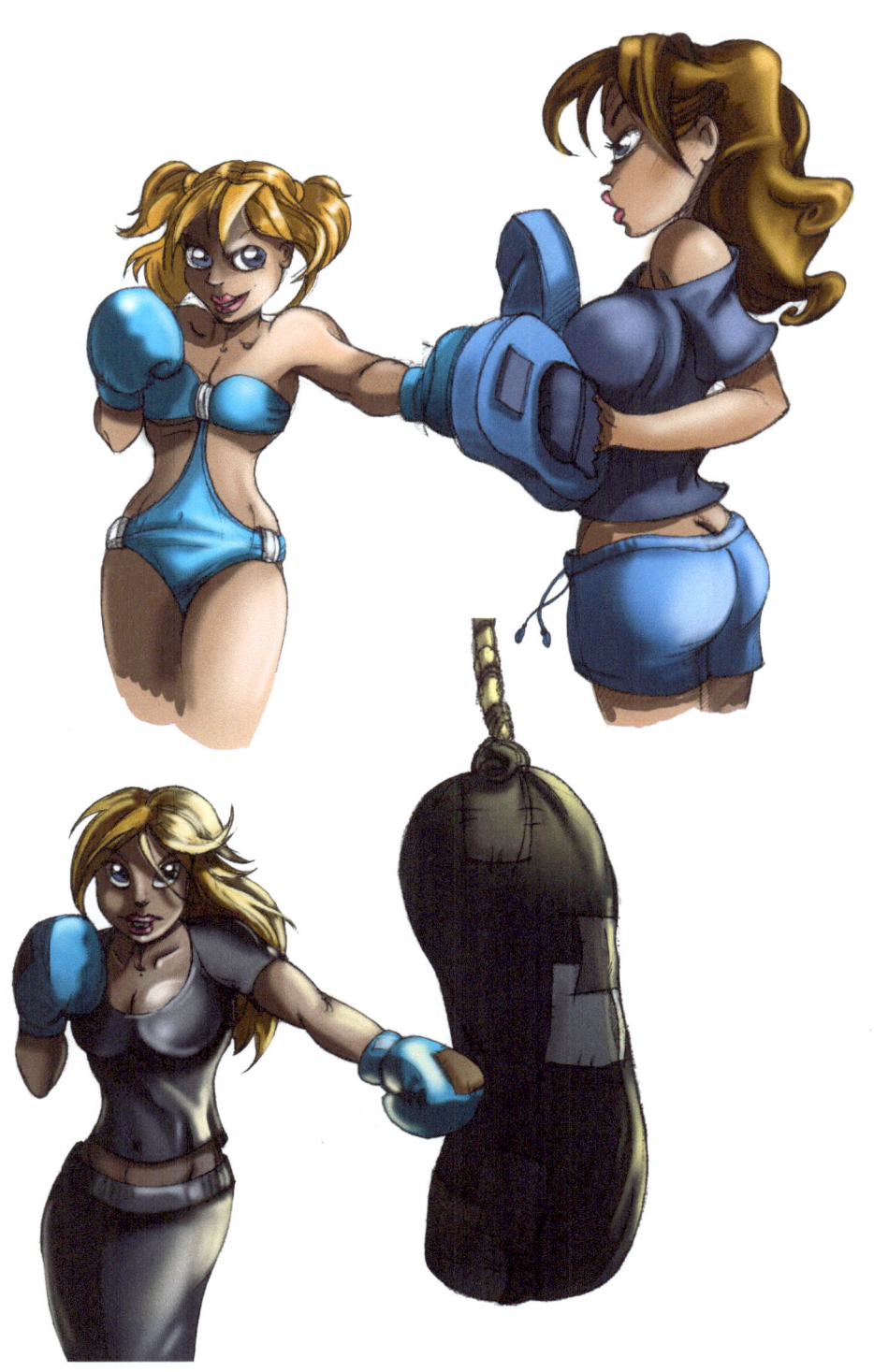

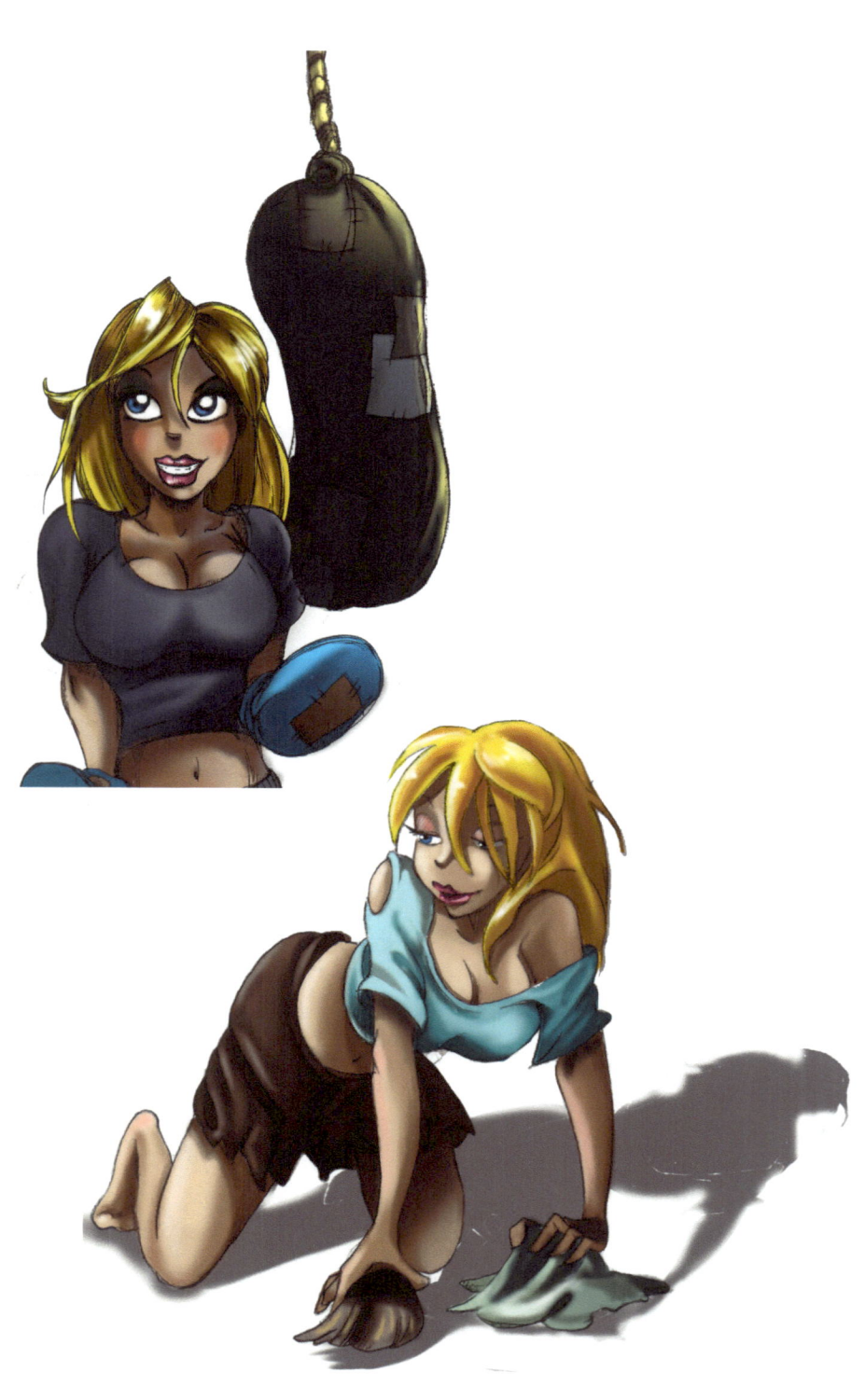

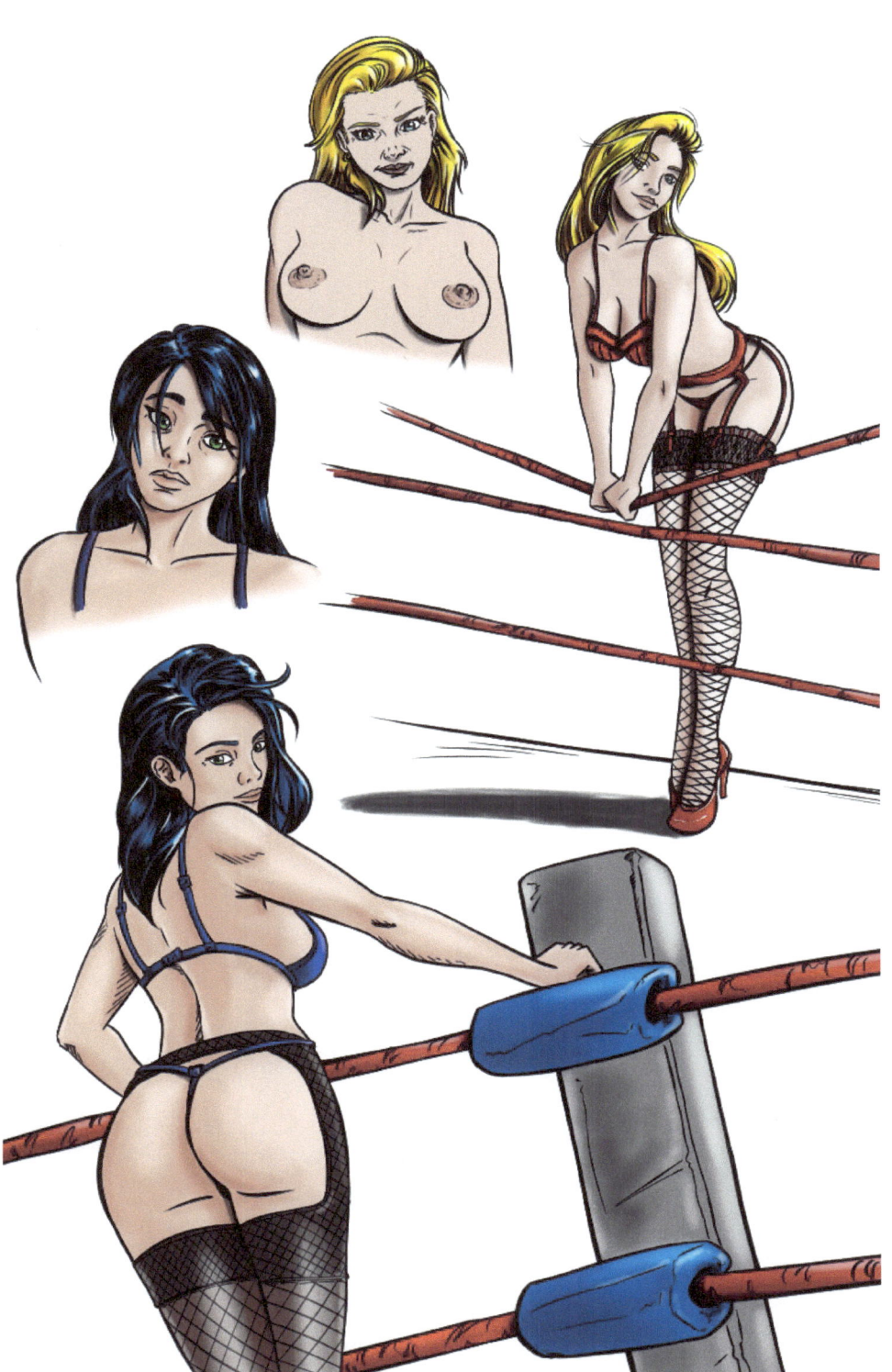

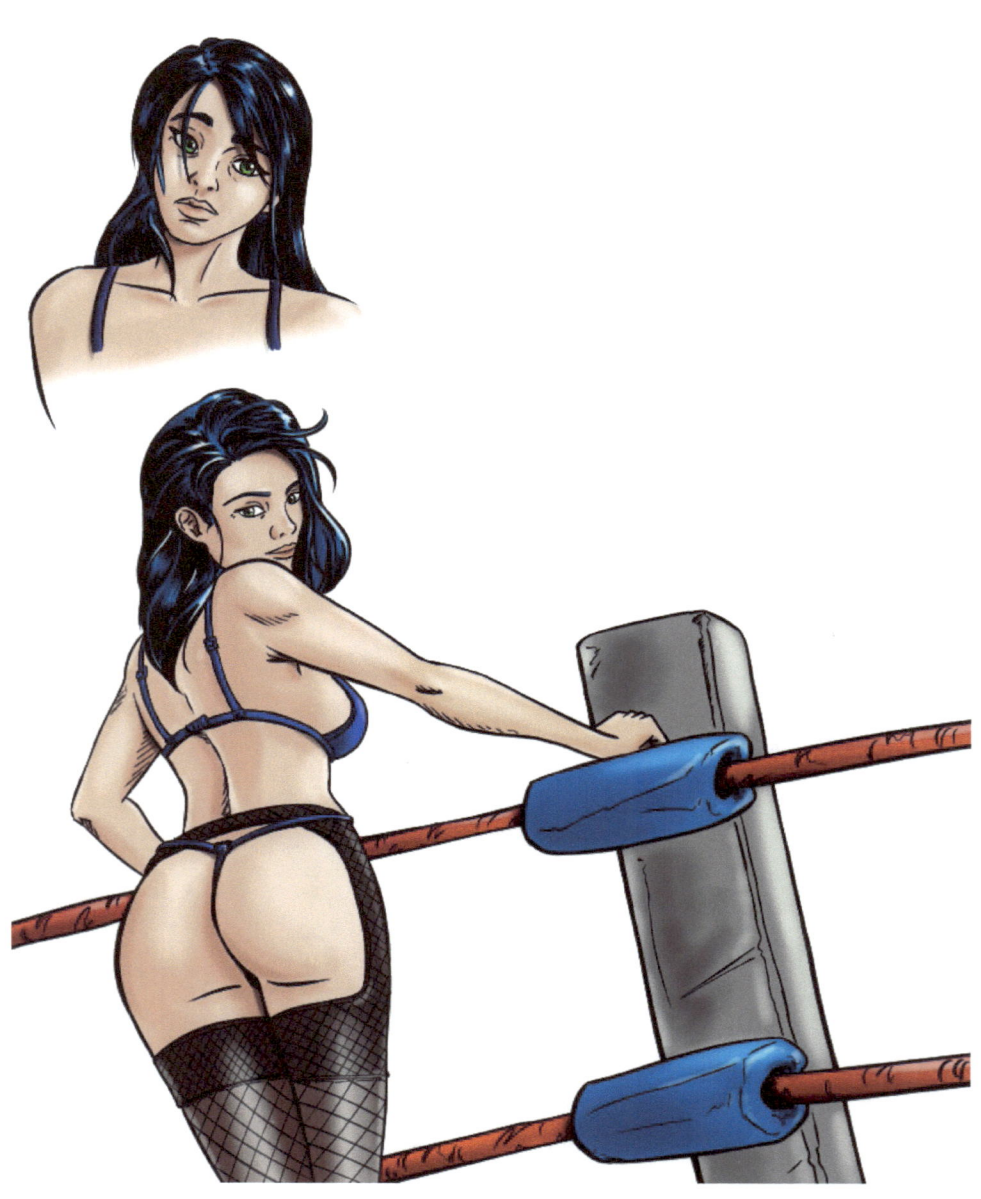

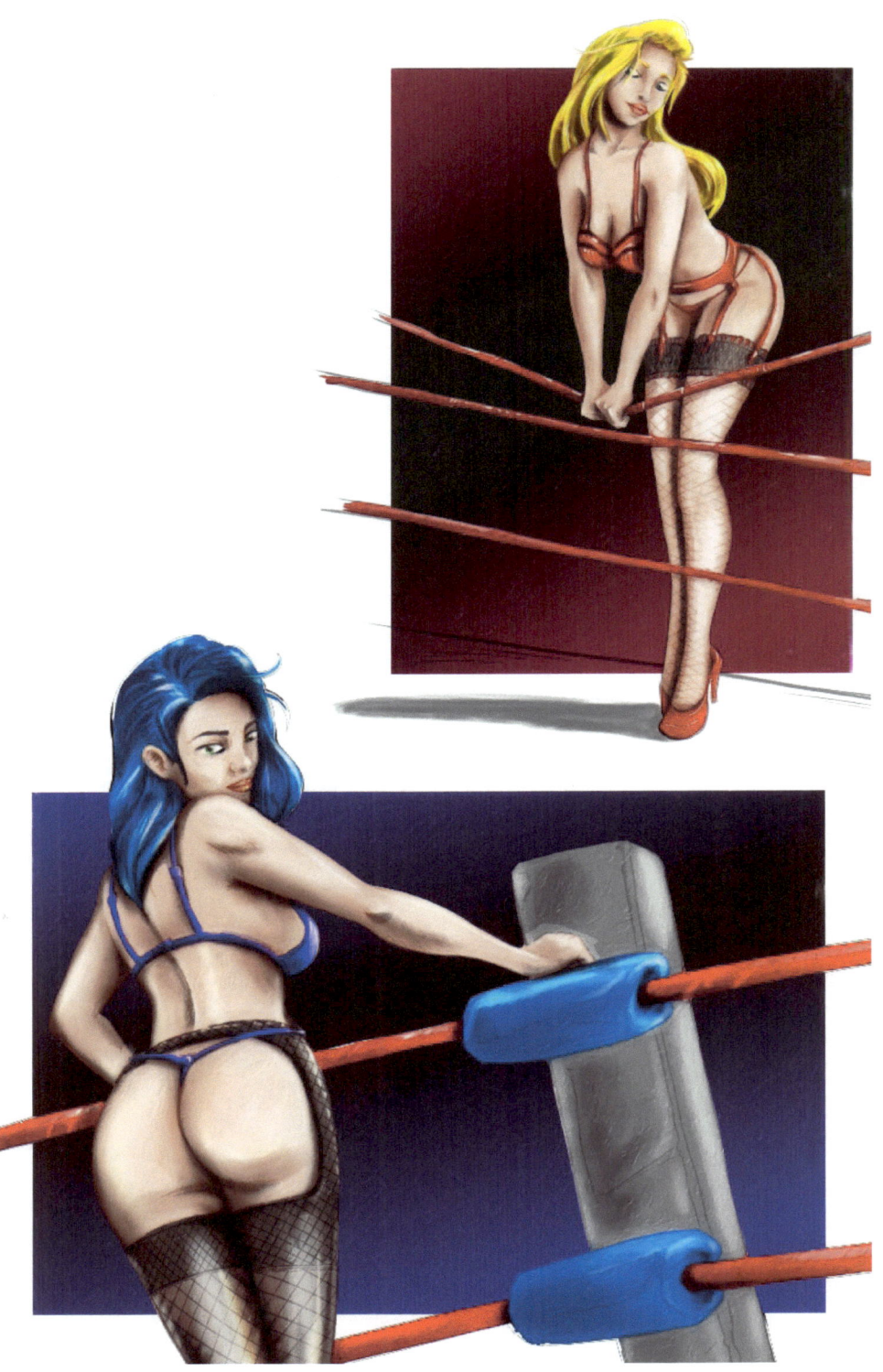

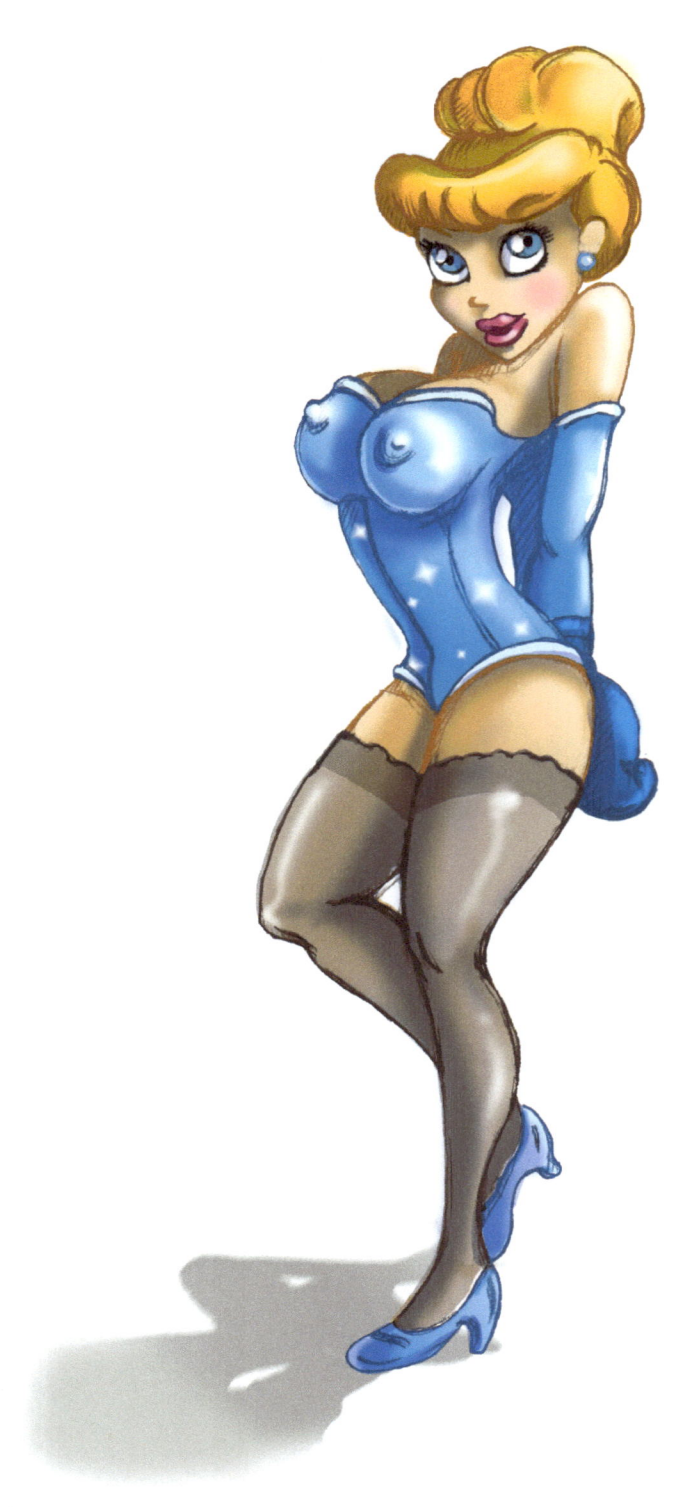

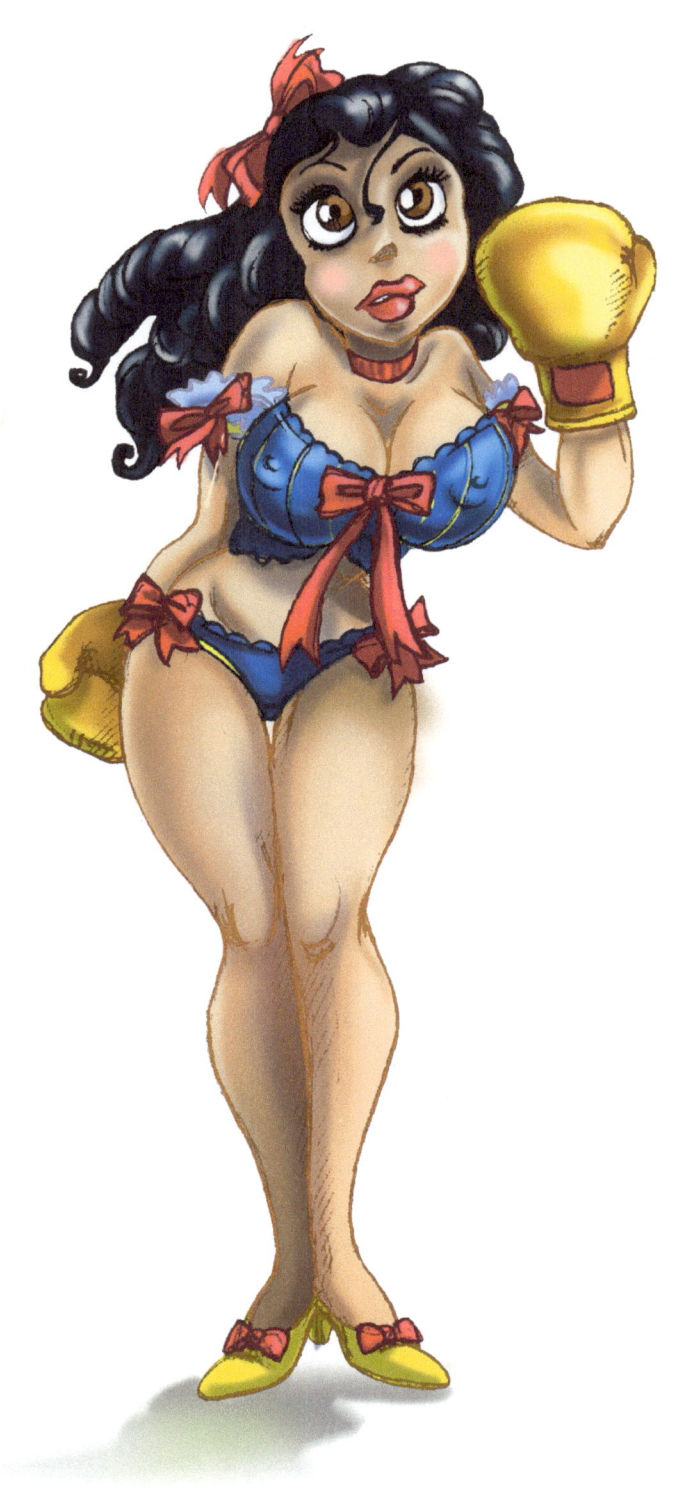

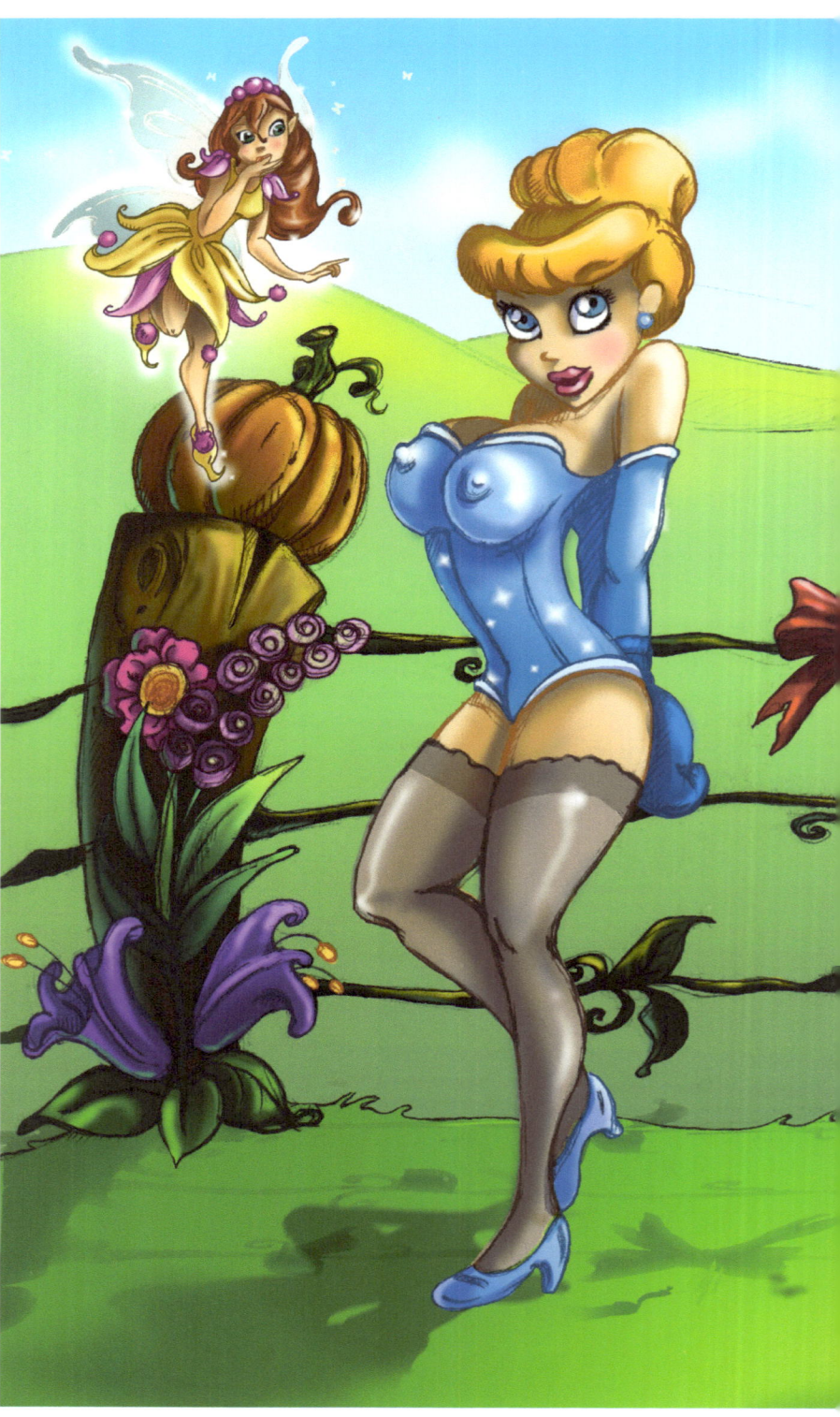

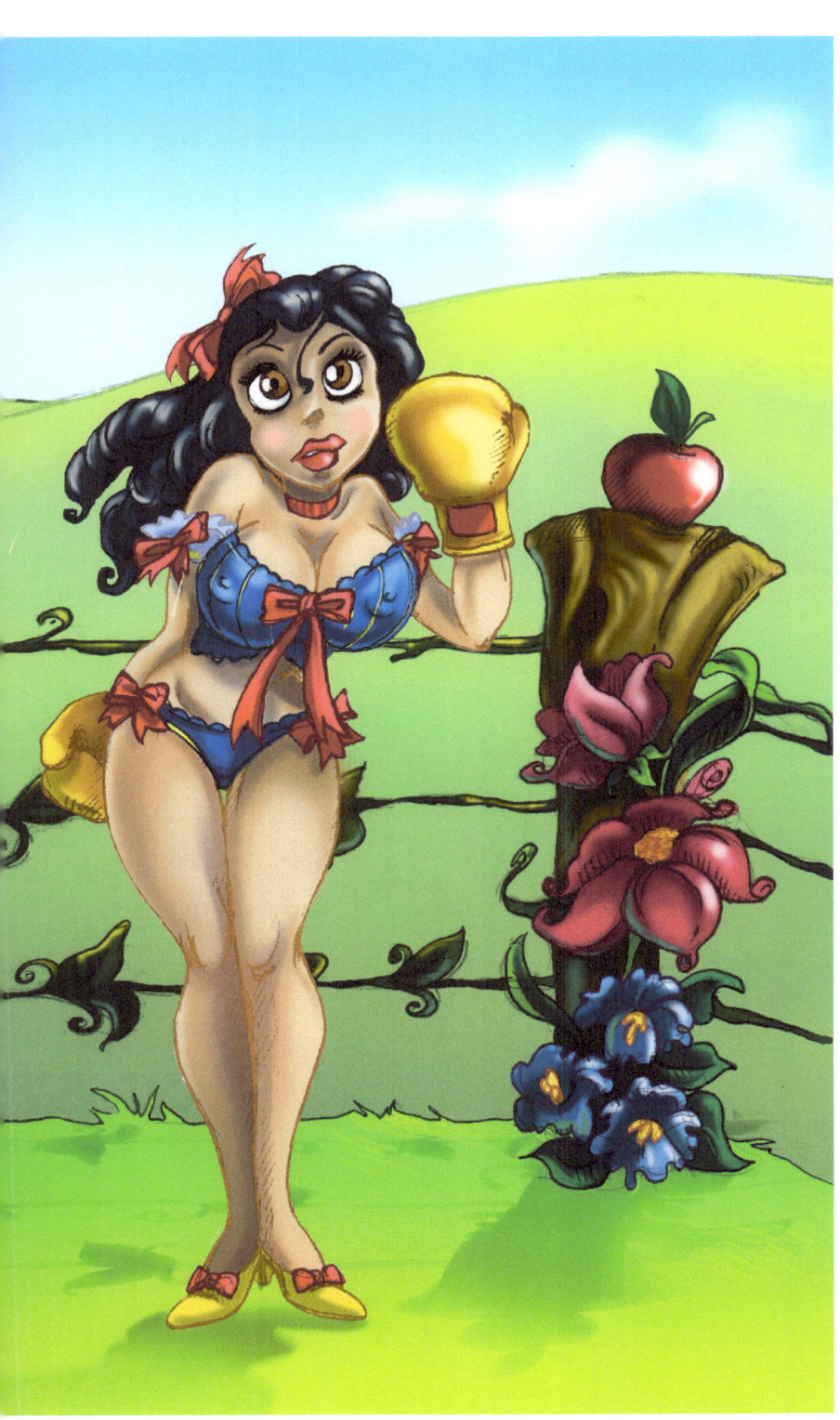

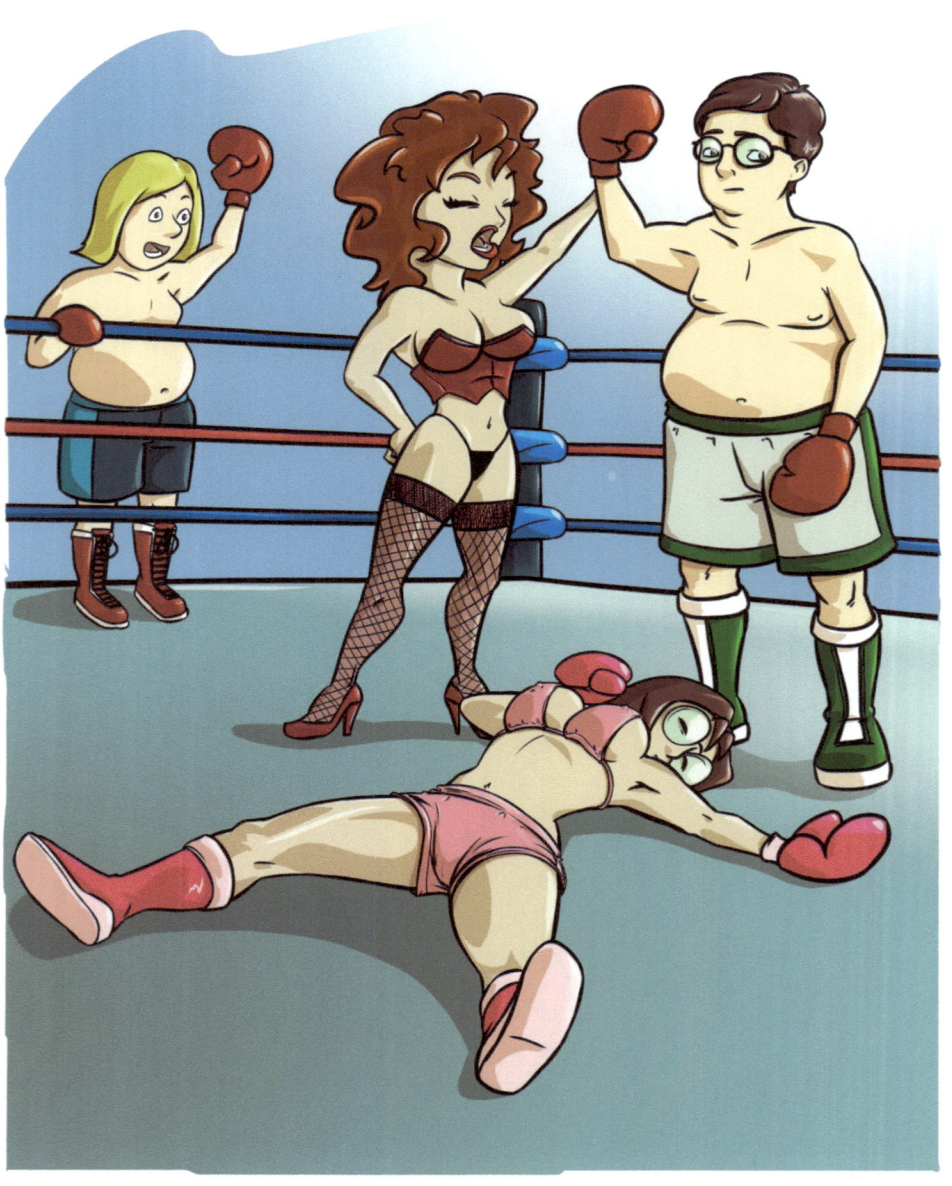

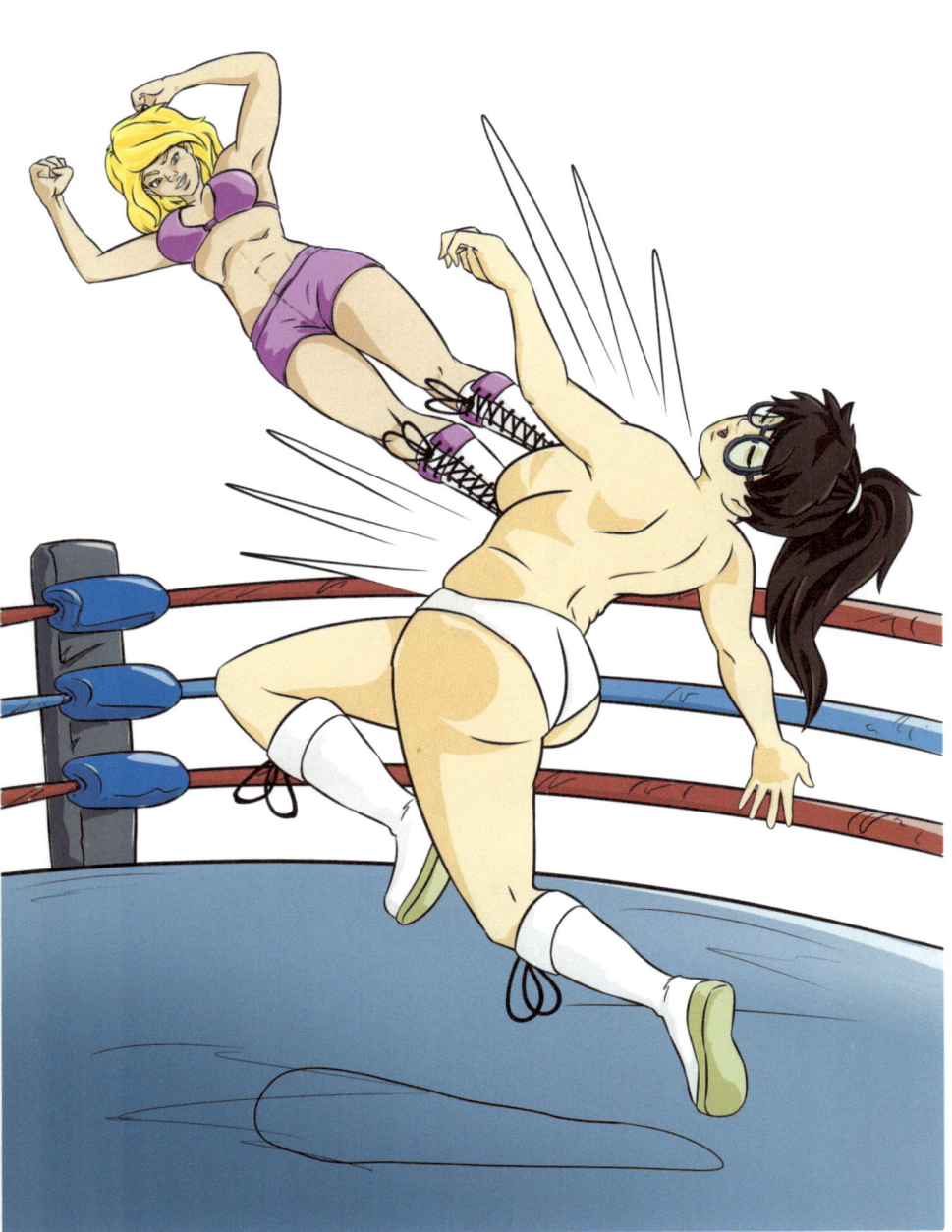

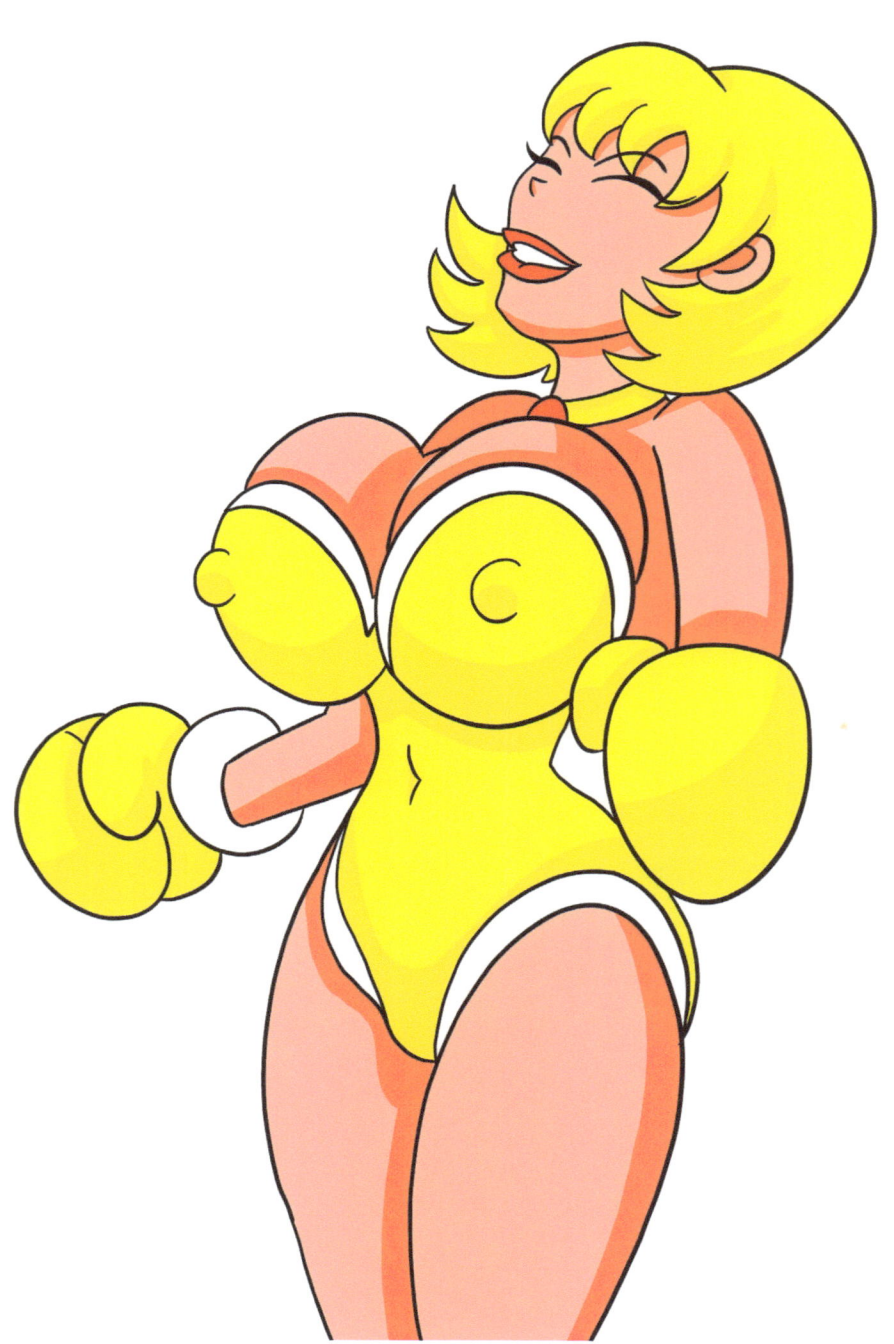

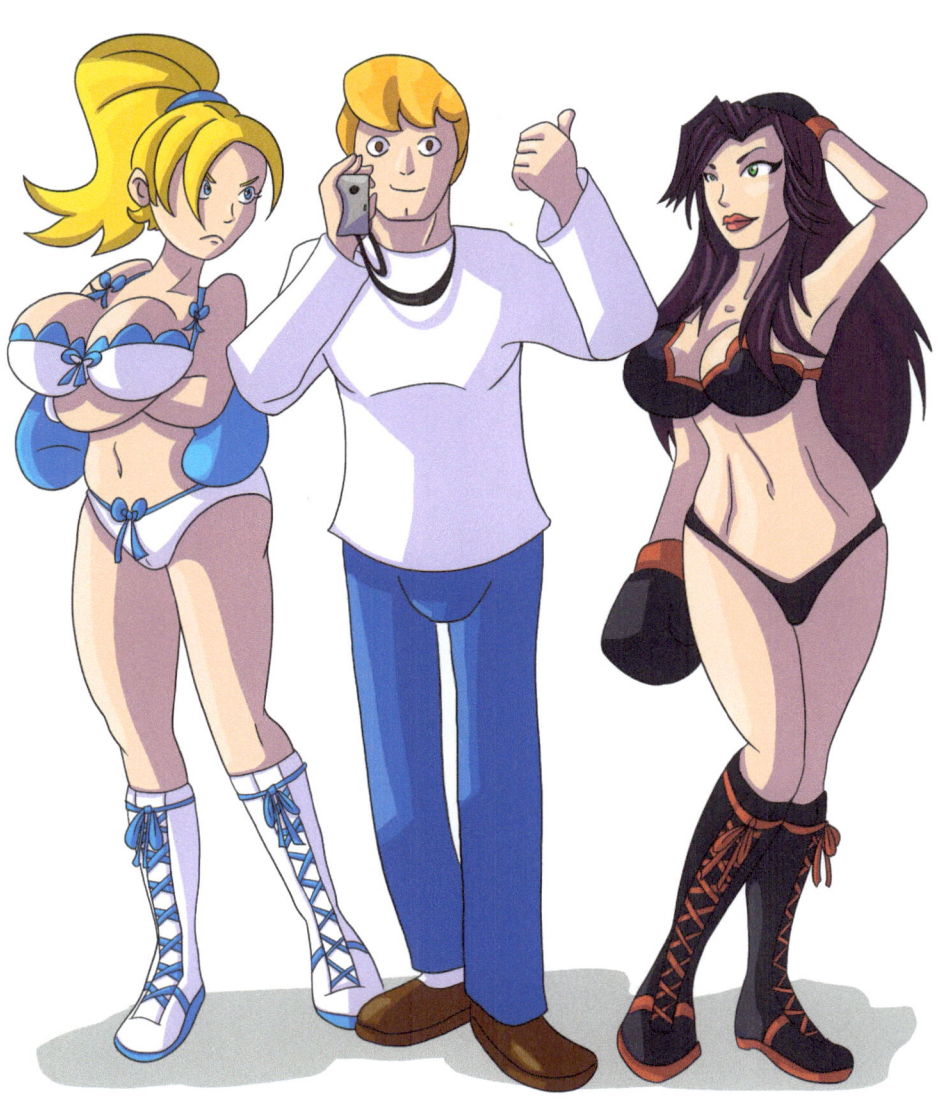

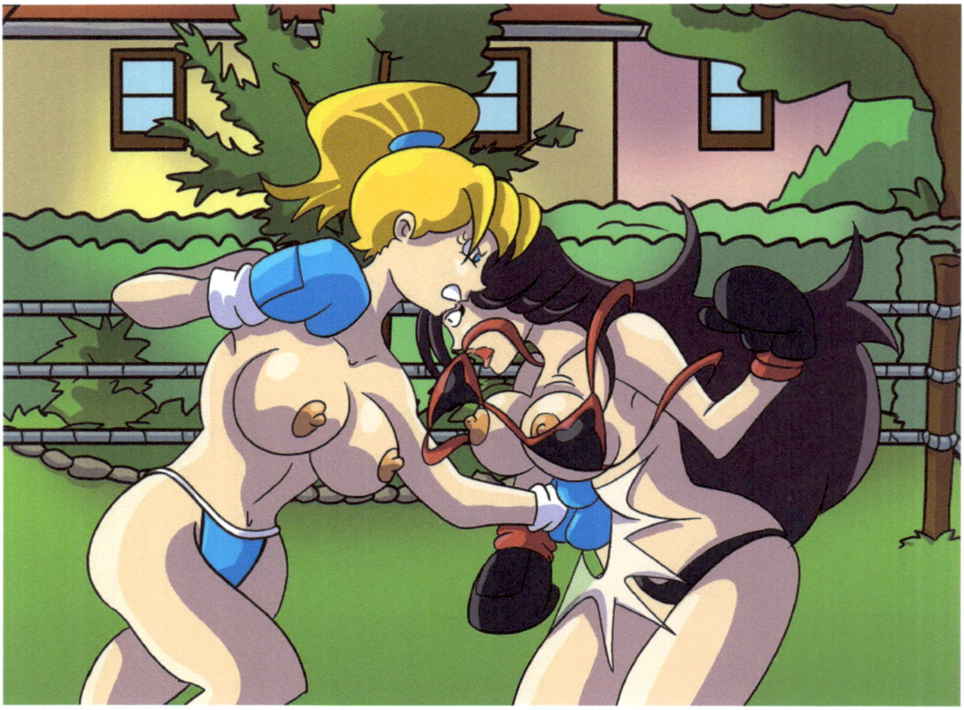

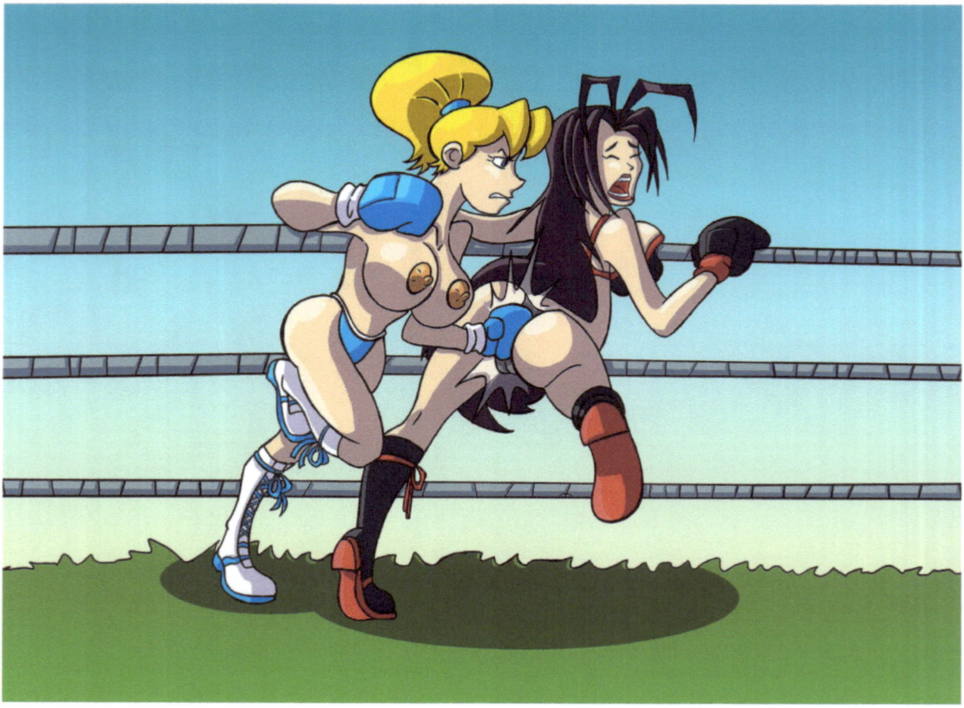

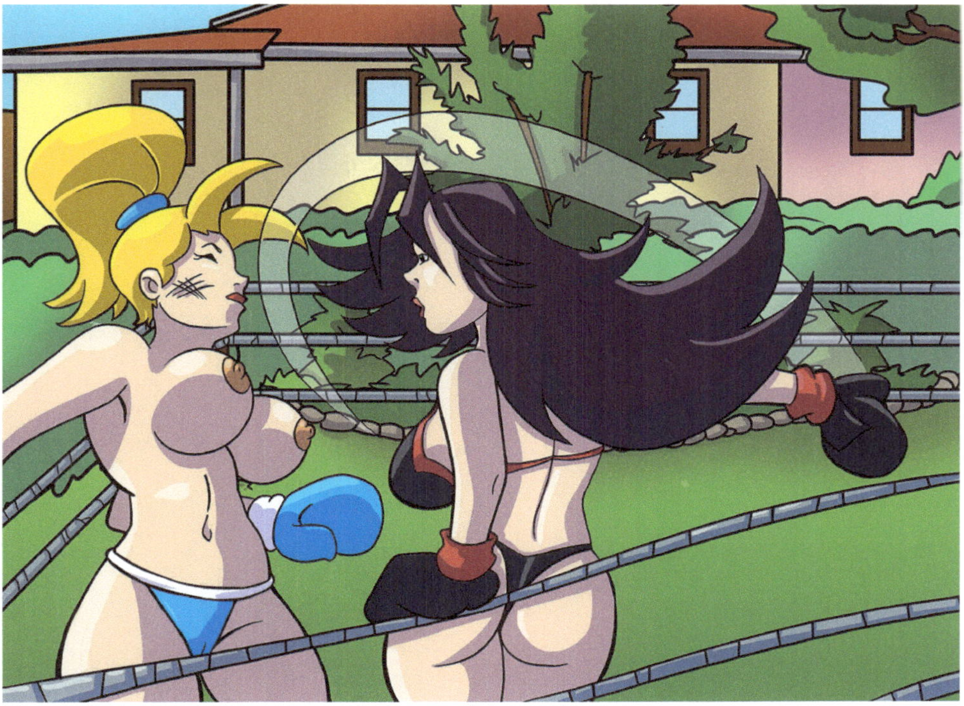

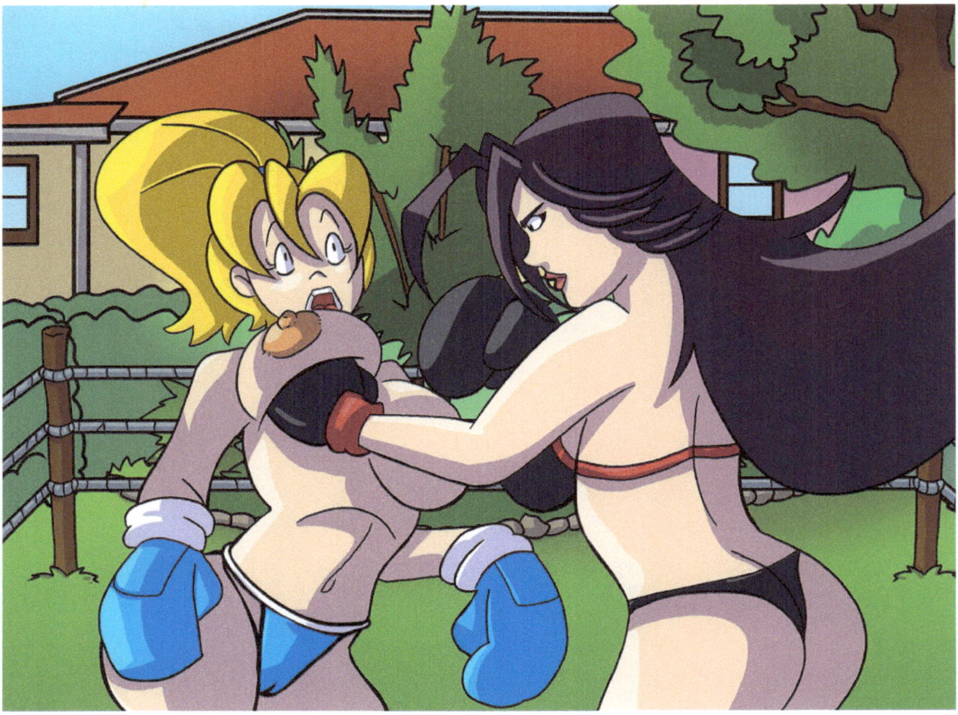

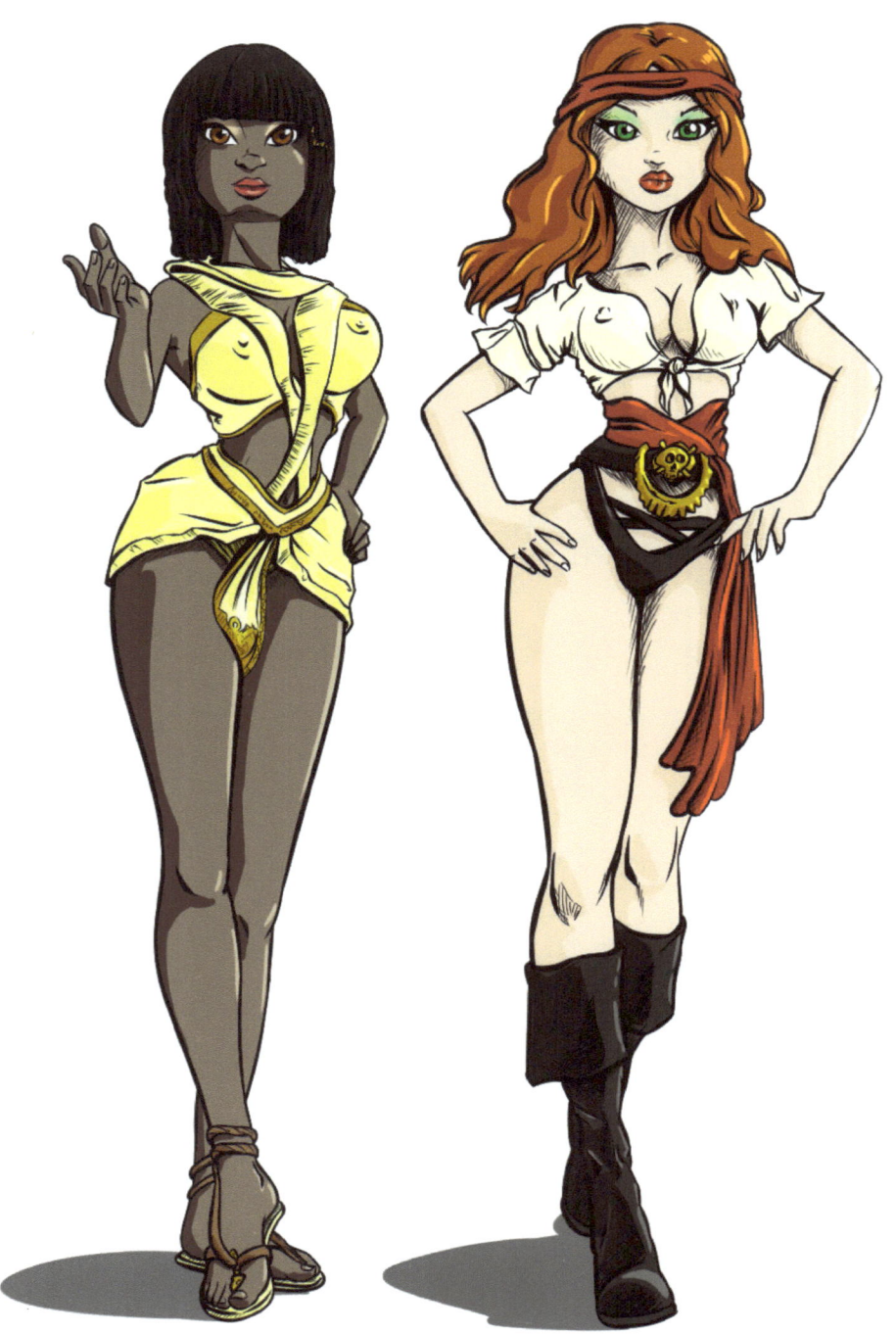

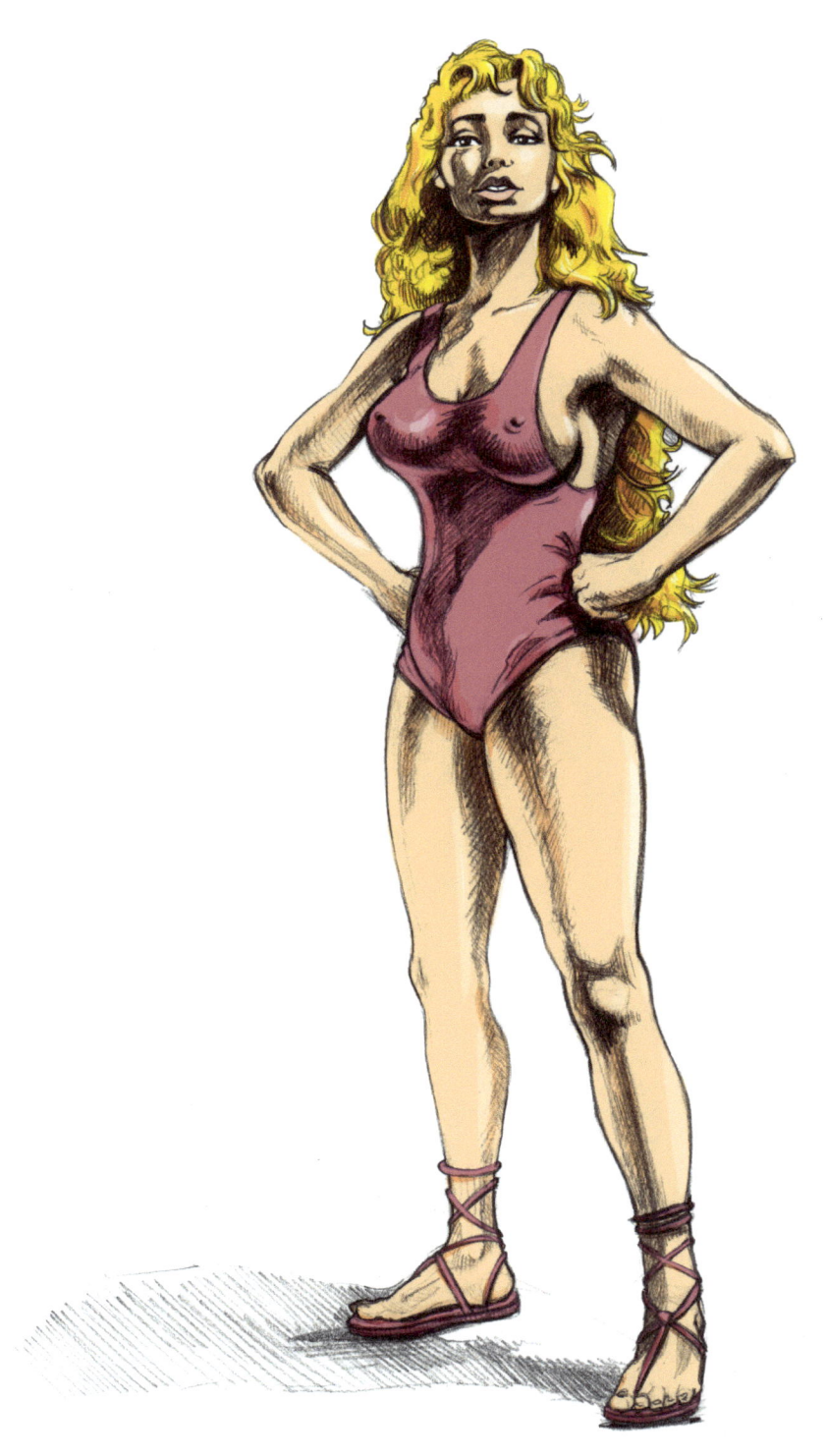

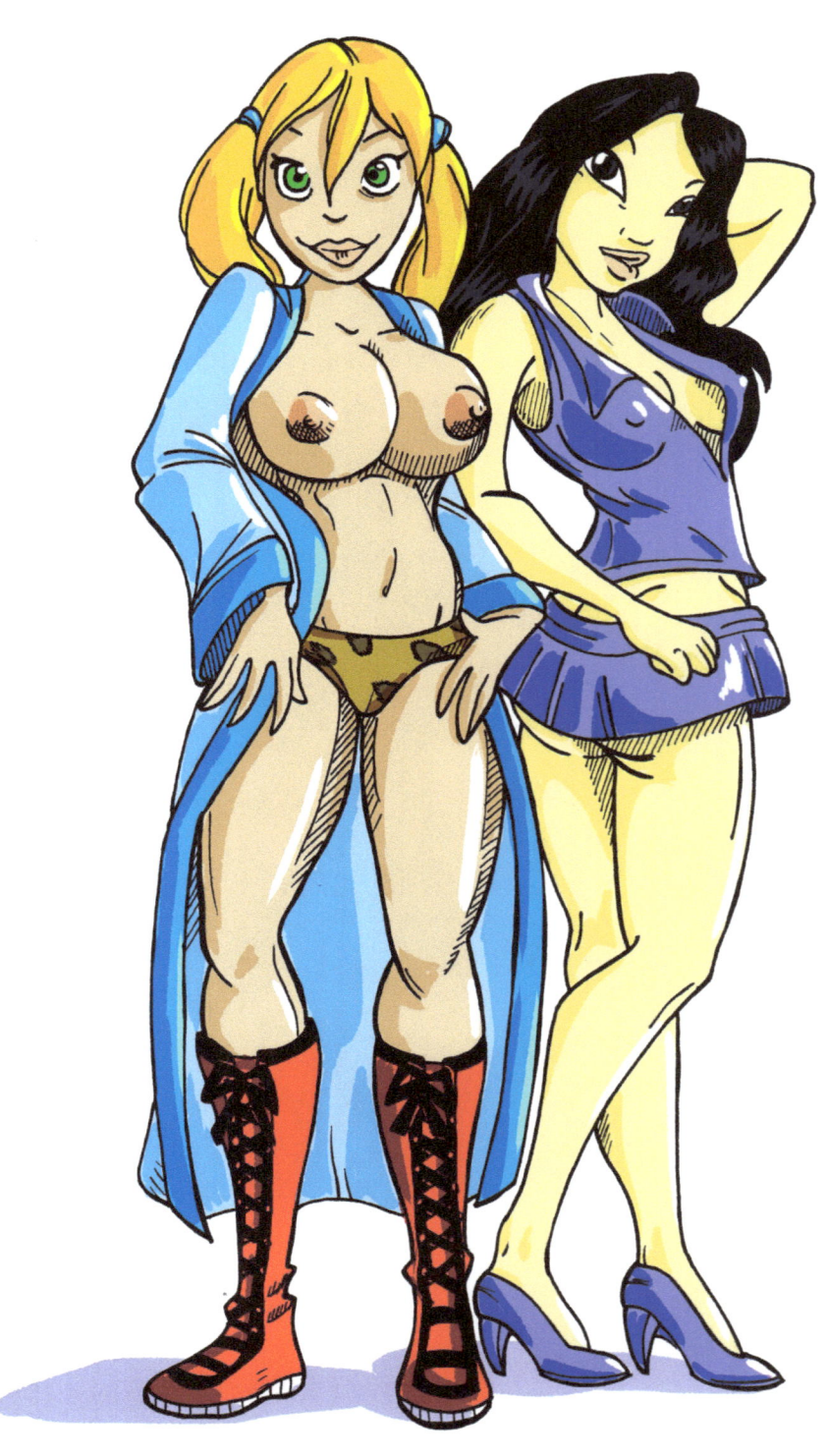

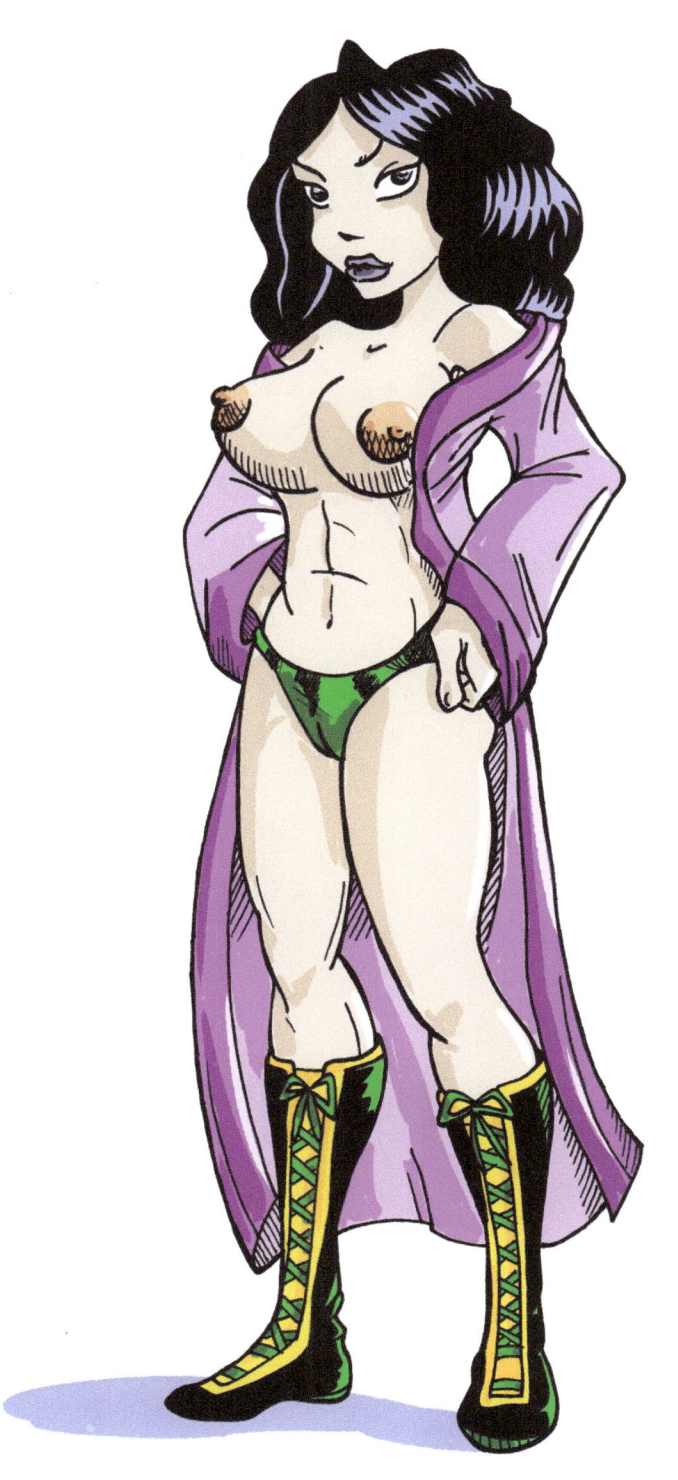

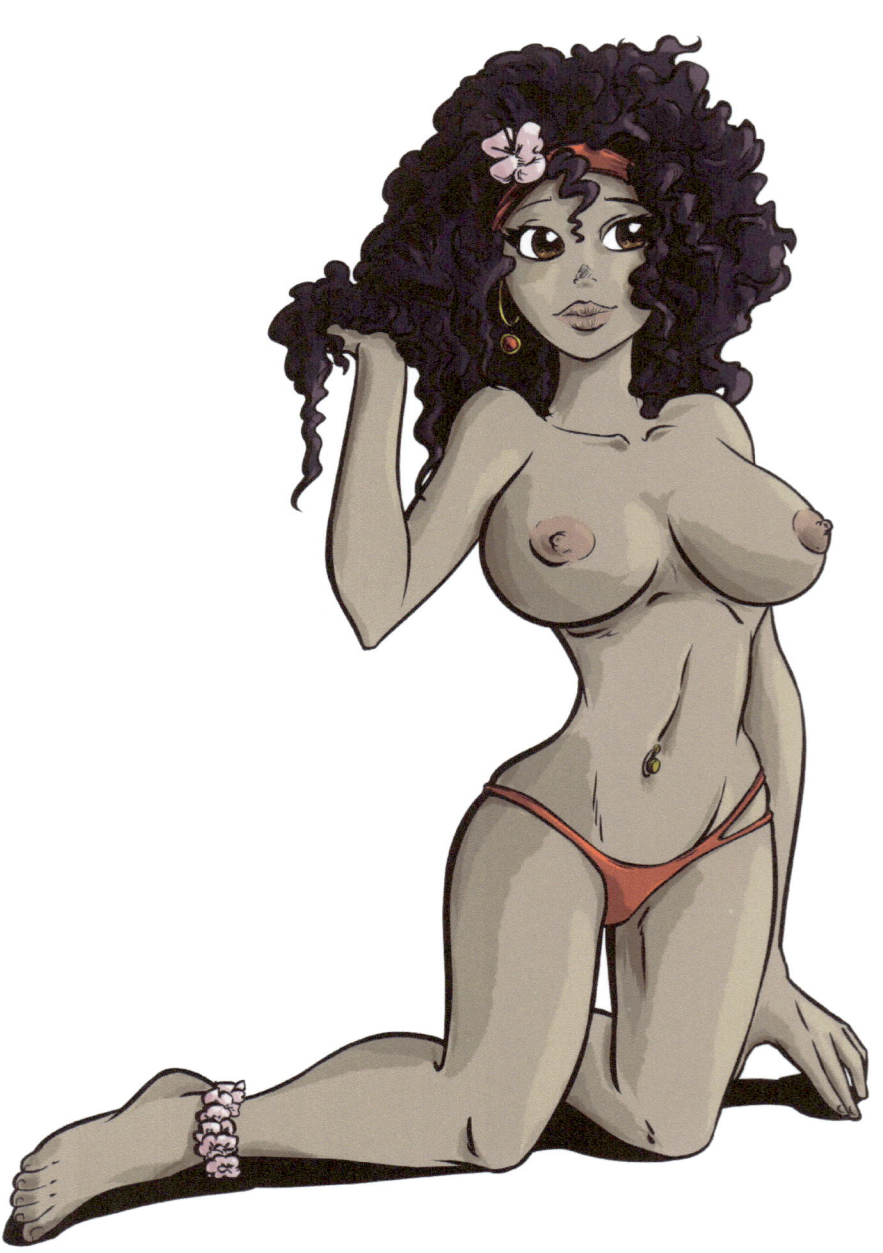

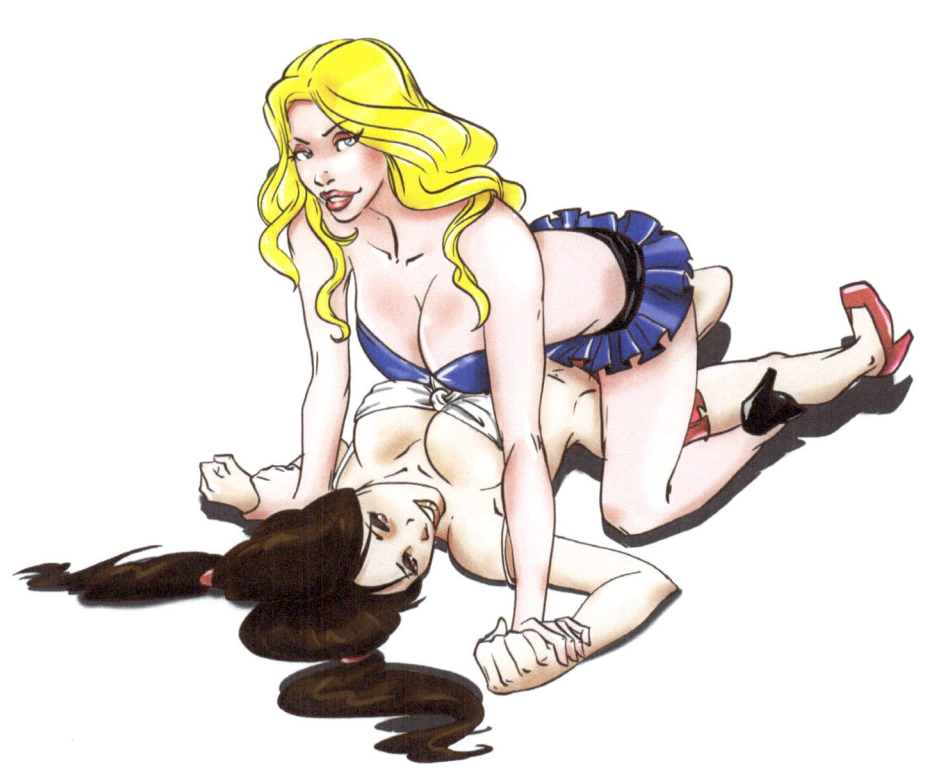

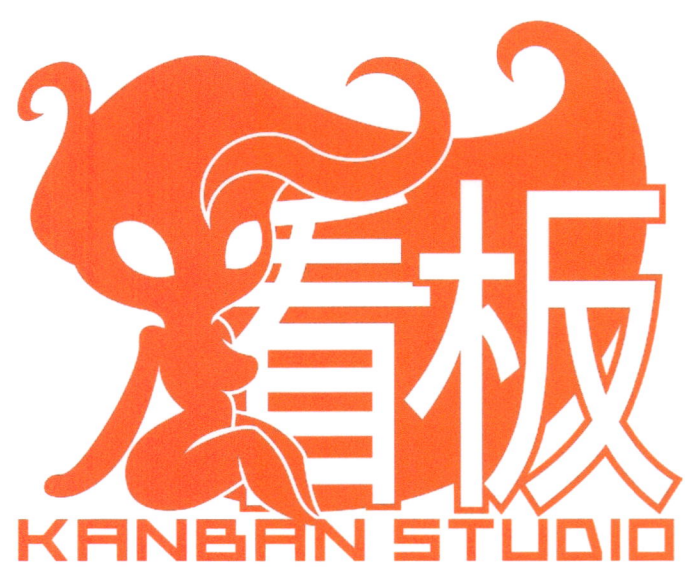

KANBAN STUDIO (KBS for short) is a hub for artists devoted to erotic art that aims at promoting top quality sensual entertainment.

The creative team is formed by writers, traditional and digital artists and covers a broad range of styles, including traditional European eroticism, American good girls and manga.

http://kanbanstudio.blogspot.com/

www.ingramcontent.com/pod-product-compliance
Lightning Source LLC
Chambersburg PA
CBHW040241220526
45473CB00001B/332